COLLABORATIVE LEADERSHIP
AND
SHARED DECISION MAKING

TEACHERS,
      PRINCIPALS, AND
            UNIVERSITY PROFESSORS

COLLABORATIVE LEADERSHIP AND SHARED DECISION MAKING

TEACHERS,
PRINCIPALS, AND
UNIVERSITY PROFESSORS

Renee T. Clift
Mary Lou Veal
Patricia Holland
Marlene Johnson
Jane McCarthy

Forewords by
Frances S. Bolin
and Peter T. Wilson

TEACHERS
COLLEGE
PRESS

Teachers College, Columbia University
New York and London

Published by Teachers College Press, 1234 Amsterdam Avenue, New York, NY 10027

Copyright © 1995 by Teachers College, Columbia University

Library of Congress Cataloging-in-Publication Data

Collaborative leadership and shared decision making : teachers,
    principals, and university professors / Renee T. Clift . . . [et al.].
            p.   cm.
        Includes bibliographical references (p.) and index.
        ISBN 0-8077-3394-6 (alk. paper). — ISBN 0-8077-3393-8 (pbk. :
    alk. paper)
        1. College-school cooperation—United States—Case studies.
    2. Educational leadership—United States—Case studies. 3. Teacher
    participation in administration—United States—Case studies.
    4. Action research in education—United States—Case studies.
    5. School principals—United States—Case studies. 6. Teacher
    educators—United States—Case studies.   I. Clift, Renee Tipton.
    LB2331.53.C64   1995
    378.1'03—dc20   94-23381
                            OCLC: 31045273

ISBN 0-8077-3393-8 (paper)
ISBN 0-8077-3394-6 (cloth)

Printed on acid-free paper
Manufactured in the United States of America

02 01 00 99 98 97 96 95   8 7 6 5 4 3 2 1

Contents

Foreword

Frances S. Bolin

In *Collaborative Leadership and Shared Decision Making: Teachers, Principals, and University Professors,* Renee T. Clift, Mary Lou Veal, Patricia Holland, Marlene Johnson, and Jane McCarthy describe a model of school-university collaboration which they term *professional reflective activity.* Professional reflective activity involves the kind of messy, entangled, and unending work that occurs when a diverse group of people enter into a common enterprise. While interests of group participants may appear to overlap—and usually do to some extent—their goals, visions, and needs are unlikely to be the same. This book illustrates how participants in a 3-year school-university partnership attempted to make progress in the face of the inevitable conflict that occurs when there is a rigorous and honest effort to be inclusive of diversity without compromising individual integrity.

Discussions of school-university partnerships are not new. The word *collaboration* crowds our professional literature around discussions of teacher empowerment, school governance, professional development schools, and restructuring. The professional development schools movement, as one example, is beginning to generate a rich literature of its own on school and university collaboration. While new and exciting, professional development schools harken to the earlier Trainers of Trainers of Teachers projects of the late 1960s where model schools were created—schools where university and school people came together to develop a more powerful preservice education experience. These, of course, were preceded by laboratory schools; and before these by Normal Schools which focused on professional practice. Movements focusing on school-university partnership spring up periodically, generating a flurry of interest and fading as new movements replace them. With each new movement there are usually descriptions by key participants with generalizations useful for others engaged in similar activity; but until recently, there has been little theoretical work around which serious scholarly discussion can occur. Without such discussions, we must continue to encounter otherwise avoidable pitfalls and blunders.

What commends *Collaborative Leadership and Shared Decision Making* is not only its documentation of a school-university partnership, but also its exploration of the multiple layers of meaning embedded in reflection, collaboration, and involvement with school improvement. The authors thoughtfully wonder about

the discontinuity between personal belief and professional action that is stimulated by common efforts of school teachers, administrators, and university professors. They accept the painful task of constantly deconstructing their own attitudes, values, and patterns of behavior. Their work provides insight into the
complexity of partnerships—a complexity of which few of us are unaware, but
which few of us understand.

The authors define collaboration as an agreement to work together toward a
common goal. While participants may agree upon a goal at the outset, however,
their unique understandings of that goal may not be in accord. Collaboration is an
unsettling activity for those who require certainty and need to have clearly defined goals at the outset of a project, especially because the process of collaboration may involve a redirection of goals as participants come to understand differences and as new ideas emerge. Without a calculated understanding of the tensions
inherent in a democratic, collaborative process, one can suffer from anxiety, frustration, and disillusionment as the ground on which one has firmly positioned
oneself seems to shift more often than settle.

Each participant "comes to the table" as a co-equal, not as the representative
of a stereotype. That is, participants will bring with them unique experiences,
perceptions of reality, and deeply held values—including habits and beliefs about
how to deal with conflict—which may or may not match those of other participants. At the same time, each participant carries a symbolic role that contains both
personal expectations of the ways that "classroom teachers" or "professors" themselves are supposed to think and behave, as well as expectations of the role of
"classroom teacher" and "professor" held by other participants. The same may be
said for each participant in the process. Each carries the tensions of representing
self and others who are not at the table. Furthermore, expertise resides in different persons around the table. Not all will share the same levels of expertise in any
area, despite the fact that the symbolic role one holds may carry with it an implied
expertise. A commitment to draw forth the expertise of self and other participants,
to represent self and colleagues not at the table, produces conflict that is rarely
understood and acknowledged.

Positive collaboration occurs when one brings oneself to the table with the
awful possibility that one just might change. Participants often enter into collaboration with idea that the need for change resides in the others at the table. University professors see the need for teachers and school administrators to change.
Teachers see the need for university professors and school administrators to
change, and so on. Perhaps the most dishonored members of university-school
partnerships are teacher educators, who are often forced to accept displaced rage
from teachers and administrators. This rage comes from disappointment in the
profession and is inextricably linked to internalized public images of teaching as
a demeaned profession. When teacher educators allow themselves to be victimized, they neither solve the problem of teacher rage nor do they contribute as co-

equals in a collaborative process. Until *every* participant offers his or her best thinking with an openness to the possibility that he or she could change, rather than focusing on how others should change, collaboration is unlikely to be sustained over time. Or if sustained, it will be a collaborative charade in which participants appear to make all the right moves, but subconsciously work together to prevent progress through negative cooperation.

Collaborative Leadership and Shared Decision Making illustrates how, through each step along the way, participants must talk with each other, develop common experience and understanding, and create a shared language that captures meanings that are similar enough to allow consensus. The authors describe a transforming experience, pointing to a process that evolved over the three years of the project; their detailed description suggests how multiple and complex were the ways in which transformation occurs. They describe a blurring of roles, while a distinctive image of each participant remained. They speak of respect for the work of the other without a desire to change places, and of the difficulty in creating structures that will last beyond funding. Structural issues are more complicated than provision of time issues—though having a time to reflect is crucial. Structural issues extend into the continuities and discontinuities of individual versus group needs. The authors speak of the "agonizingly slow" process of coming to trust, and of the necessity of reflecting *with* others rather than *on* them.

Given the difficulty and complexity of collaboration, one might ask, "Why? Why bother?" The book is a persuasive testimony to the value of teachers, administrators, and university professors investing time in working together. Beyond this, children and young people are deeply influenced by adult role models. The difficult, ambiguous, and uncertain work that we do in collaborating with each other not only benefits ourselves, but also provides a model of a better way for students to deal with the vagaries and vicissitudes of life in an increasingly complex world.

Foreword

Peter T. Wilson

Collaborative Leadership and Shared Decision Making provides us with a treasure lode of insights about the difficult and essential work of school/university collaboration. There are rich veins of insight regarding leadership by teachers, principals, and university faculty and how these groups interact. The analysis of several modes of reflective practice yields a useful demarcation between action research and the authors' eventual choice of Argyris, Putnam, and Smith's "action science." The authors' application and consequent examination of action science complements the work of Osterman and Kottkamp (1993).

Clift, Veal, Holland, Johnson, and McCarthy succeed in illustrating how sufficient time and persistent struggle to enable "professional reflective practice" results in professional growth for all parties, changes in school cultures, and a positive impact on students. The Time for Reflection project stimulated the emergence of "active professional learning cultures in schools." This certainly fits the findings of McLaughlin and Talbert (1993), who discovered that "professional communities . . . offer the most effective unit of intervention and powerful opportunity for reform." They see professional communities as "learning communities which generate knowledge, craft new norms of practice, and sustain participants in their efforts to reflect, examine, experiment, and change" (p. 19).

The most precious contribution by Clift et al. is the insight they provide into the struggles of teachers, principals, and professors as they attempt to develop truly collaborative work. Their struggles against the cultures of isolation, competition, and different systems of time and rewards is richly conveyed by the authors' creative combination of four conventions. They employ description, analysis, composite stories drawn from their deep body of research, and individual teacher and principal comments on these composite stories. The participants' struggle is magnified by a misguided district policy that rotates principals every 6 months and by an inflexible state-mandated teacher evaluated process.

This book is clearly organized and has a straight-forward style. The reader comes away with a deep appreciation of the essential role reflective practice must play if we are to reinvent schools that are truly learning communities. Equally important is the revealing struggle that is inevitably a part of collaborative efforts among professionals rooted in different organizational cultures. The authors do a superb job of surfacing and probing both the pains and joys of this difficult work. Anyone interested in professional development, in the emerging work of action research and reflective practice, in professional development schools and the development of learning communities will find *Collaborative Leadership and Shared Decision Making* a rich treasure.

REFERENCES

McLaughlin, M. W., & Talbert, J. E. (1993). *Contexts that matter for teaching and learning: Strategic opportunities for meeting the nation's educational goals.* Stanford, CA: Stanford University, Center for Research on the Context of Secondary School Teaching. (ERIC Document Reproduction Service No. ED 357 023)

Osterman, K. F., & Kottkamp, R. B. (1993). *Reflective practice for educators: Improving schooling through professional development.* Newbury Park, CA: Corwin.

Preface

This book explores the connections among collaborative leadership, educational inquiry, and contexts for professional learning through the story of a project called *Time for Reflection: A Project in Collaborative Leadership for Working More Effectively in Multicultural Settings*. For 3 years a group of university-based participants (the co-authors) and school practitioners worked together to create a structure and a process for collaborative leadership to enable educators in both institutions to learn about factors that facilitate continued professional learning and development. We all made a conscious choice to construct an environment in which individual goals and shared goals for school improvement were developed, given concrete form, and examined. By sharing what we have learned, we intend to contribute to current discussions of how professional educators can learn to work collaboratively across role groups and across institutions.

Our perspectives on the story of Time for Reflection, because they are written and published, are the ones that will be archived. Our responsibility, therefore, is to tell our combined interpretation of the story as honestly as possible, incorporating the voices and viewpoints of as many as possible, so that others who are teachers, principals, and university educators may learn what they will from our experiences as they, too, work toward the goals of transforming relationships among educators, as well as the structure of educational institutions. The perspective the five co-authors bring is that of friends and colleagues whose lives have been strongly affected by our experiences. We are now reflecting on the multiple meanings of those experiences as our five separate voices are combined in this text through a process of discussion, argument, negotiation, and revision to provide a university-based perspective on the relationships between professional development and collaborative leadership within and across educational institutions.

We also have struggled to include the voices of the school participants in several ways. The first and most obvious is the inclusion in Chapters 4 and 5 of commentaries written by school-based participants using their real names. The second is the numerous quotes throughout the text and the composite cases in Chapters 4 and 5 in which we have combined stories of individuals across role groups in order to protect individual identities. Less obvious is the revision based on feedback from school-based participants as we wrote and revised cases and chapters.

We gratefully acknowledge the help, the support, and the continuing friendship of the following individuals: Dianne Akins-Iglehart, Rod Dunklee, Yolande Eugere, Kyle Ferral, Sandra Ford, Becky Gill, Melanie Heasley, Jacquelyn Hinojosa, Gayle Holder, Linda Jackson, Georgia McGlasson, Patricia McLane, Ernie Ortiz, Sherry Roberts, Gwen Rutledge, Francene Shapiro, Dianne Lazarine Thomas, Eftimea Ulrey, Virginia Upchurch-Ditzig, Priscilla Watkins, Erin Welch, and Janice Young.

We would also like to thank our students, friends, colleagues, and families who patiently read chapter drafts and listened to us say, "We have to get this book finished," more times than we had a right to expect. Thank you Bonnie Armbruster, Prentice Baptiste, Kate Barrett, Lana Bates, Bertram Bruce, June Chambliss, Myrna Craig, Bill Georgiades, Bob Houston, Susan Noffke, Sarah M. Robinson, and Inez Rovegno. Special thanks to Patt Dodds for her careful reading and thoughtful critique. The University of North Carolina at Greensboro provided support to Mary Lou in the form of a Summer Research Grant, from which we all benefitted.

The people at the Danforth Foundation who believed in us, funded the original project, and then helped us bring school-based participants back together to read, critique, and help write this text made our work possible and gave us advice and guidance throughout the project: Bruce Anderson, Donn Gresso, and Peter Wilson.

Our editors at Teachers College Press gave us support during all of the times we wanted to quit writing. They counseled us, without ever expressing disappointment or anger, through our personal traumas and triumphs, our moves from the University of Houston to other positions, and our numerous revisions of chapters and formats. Sarah Biondello and Susan Liddicoat are the two main reasons this book ever reached publication.

Finally, we want to dedicate this book to two people who touched (and continue to touch) our lives and our work, but whose untimely deaths prevented their seeing this book through to completion: Debra Powers, a middle school English teacher, and Ron Galbraith, our original TCP editor.

COLLABORATIVE LEADERSHIP
AND
SHARED DECISION MAKING

TEACHERS,
 PRINCIPALS, AND
  UNIVERSITY PROFESSORS

CHAPTER 1

Learning from Research and Practice

In most departments of psychology and schools of education, teaching continues as though nothing had happened and the quest for immutable objective truths were as promising as ever. For some of us, however, a different view of knowledge *has* emerged, not as a new invention but rather as a result of pursuing suggestions made by much earlier dissidents. This view differs from the old one in that it deliberately discards the notion that knowledge could or should be a representation of an observer-independent world-in-itself and replaces it with the demand that the conceptual constructs we call knowledge be *viable* in the experiential world of the knowing subject. (Ernst Von Glaserfeld, 1989, p. 122)

To read about what is wrong with education in the United States, one need only open a newspaper or watch the television news. Both the popular press and the academic press routinely supply information cataloguing the failures of teachers, schools, administrators, university professors, parents, and politicians to provide proper educational opportunities for children and young adults. Frequently, these accounts are followed by prescriptions for reform—more money, less money; school choice, rebuilding neighborhood schools; greater teacher autonomy, more restrictions on curriculum and instruction; and so forth. Within the rhetoric one message is very clear: the institution of education is under constant scrutiny and attack from people within the education profession *and* from those who do not work in this field. Many of these critics, whose opinions and values are often in opposition to one another, appeal to (presumably) expert knowledge as they offer deceptively simple solutions for complex problems. Such a climate of educational criticism was the norm in 1987 when we began working on Time for Reflection (TFR), a project in collaborative leadership for working more effectively in multicultural settings. It is still the norm today as we write and revise this book in 1994.

It is our opinion that while discussion and criticism are both healthy and necessary, too many critics are more interested in finding fault or promoting a particular ideology than in accepting responsibility for working toward solutions with those who are directly connected with students on a daily basis. Those who are most often charged with implementing external solutions—public school teachers and administrators, university-based teacher educators and administrative educators, students themselves—are often left out of the public conversation. Rather, they debate among themselves as they explicate an assumption that they are powerless to change the policy, the critics, or themselves. But this is not true for all educators everywhere. Some educators, as individuals and in groups, are actively working against the assumption that solutions can or should be imposed from without. For such people, who have incomplete road maps to chart change efforts, living with the ambiguity and uncertainty that accompany side roads, wrong turns, and poor driving conditions is becoming an accepted component of the task of education.

This book describes a 3-year relationship among a group of educators who worked from within to understand better the task of school improvement and to begin the process of making individual changes as well as schoolwide changes. Our story will not be one more account of educational failure, nor do we offer a fairy tale in which all the protagonists live happily ever after. What we describe is a joint struggle among educators in five public schools and one university to learn more about working together to improve professional learning environments. During this struggle we also came to learn more about our respective educational roles and about ourselves. In telling our story, the five co-authors of this book and the school participants who have contributed to the text offer our collective insights to other educators who are committed to creating environments that enable people across institutions and role designations to work together to define issues, identify problems, and move toward greater understanding of potential solutions.

We begin the story by describing the events that enabled the participants to come together and begin to reach consensus about the design and scope of TFR. In so doing we discuss our evolving conceptions of learning from experience and research. In Chapter 2 we describe how we came to view school–university relationships that combine intervention with support for school-designed projects, as we describe the methods used to collect and analyze data with and for (as well as about) project participants. In subsequent chapters we elaborate and extend the project story line for each school and for the project as a whole. Although this book is the story of one project, it is at the same time an intersection of individual stories of the prospective teachers, practicing teachers, school administrators, graduate students, and university professors who worked with Time for Reflection. While the co-authors' voices are predominant, we have included the voices of the school participants through quotes, their own writing, and our many revisions based on their feedback. We have learned much through our continuous interactions with one another—and we remain aware that we have much more to learn.

A METAPHOR FOR LEARNING
THROUGH COLLABORATIVE RESEARCH

In the eighteenth and nineteenth centuries many middle-class homes in England and the United States had parlors—rooms at the front of the house reserved for guests. In such spaces servants or housewives did not need to scurry around picking up after the children if company called, for children were not allowed into these areas without special permission. While childhood friends might be permitted to visit in the kitchen, the playroom, or perhaps even the bedrooms, all understood that friends' parents were not to be escorted into the living areas. A polite fiction was maintained by inhibiting a public acknowledgment that the household was not as orderly, or as grand, as the parlor area might imply. At the same time, family members were able to conduct daily routines without interference from unexpected guests. Social distance was maintained for practical convenience as well as to maintain social appearances.

Often, there is a parallel concept of parlor space in educational research. In what we might term the parlor tradition, a certain group of researchers seek to study aspects of schooling without becoming personally involved in the school context. Public and private areas of teaching, administration, and research are carefully maintained, particularly those areas related to the private world of the researcher-guests. Carefully constructed interviews, surveys, and scheduled observations provide information that such educational researchers find both interesting and useful, as they seek to remain objective and apart from the people and places they study.

A second group of researchers, who also maintain a degree of social distance, may venture beyond the parlor to spend some time in the living areas, sometimes for the purpose of helping the occupants rearrange the metaphoric furniture or partially redecorate the instructional space. These researchers are sometimes invited guests; other times they are imposed on schools by others who intend to "fix" that which is judged to be "broken." Often, these researchers provide valuable advice to one or more occupants. At times, however, they become concerned and even irritated when the occupants fail to buy or to implement successfully the latest version of educational reform. Such irritation may be reciprocated by teachers and administrators who mentally write off outsiders as uncaring, unrealistic, unthoughtful, and unwelcome.

Neither the parlor guests nor the interior designers share their own worlds with the school inhabitants. Partially as a function of methodological training, these researchers exhibit only a dispassionate, public face while interacting with school personnel. Sometimes their research procedure includes the sharing of research or evaluation results with participants, but often it does not. Only researcher colleagues are invited to view and critique methodology and inference, which in our view serves to maintain a distance between research and practice. This distance is acceptable, is indeed desirable, to a number of educators, regardless of their institutional affiliation, who feel that a certain distance and objectivity are necessary for thoughtful analysis.

A third group of educational researcher-guests are taking an increasingly active interest in working with teachers, administrators, and university faculties. The researchers often seek adoption as occasional and transitory members of the family. They agree to help with the dishes, cook a few meals, and tidy up when asked to do so. They also open themselves to the family as their private worlds become somewhat intertwined with family events. If they are successful, they are granted partial entry into the experiences of everyday living. They cannot claim to be objective and unaffected by the occupants of the house, for as these researchers become more intimately connected with practice, practice informs and shapes both the research and the researchers. While we might not have labeled ourselves this way when we began Time for Reflection, the five co-authors' actions throughout our experiences and subsequent interpretations of our work place us in this third group.

We would like to emphasize that this view of educational research is not an established paradigm; rather it is being developed by those of us who are questioning the personal meaning and practical utility of earlier, more established paradigms. In the publication of her presidential address to the American Educational Research Association, Ann Lieberman (1992) noted:

> Those university researchers—whose goals are the transforming of schools and universities—find that their goals change the nature of their relationship with schools, challenging them to reevaluate the role of research and the responsibilities of researchers who participate in authentic collaboration with school-based educators. (p. 10)

Throughout this book we argue that continuous re-evaluation is healthy, desirable, and inevitable given our belief that knowledge of, for, and about teaching and learning is a dynamic, constructive process. In the next section we elaborate on this conception of learning and its effect on the design of professional education.

A CONSTRUCTIVIST VIEW OF RESEARCH AND PRACTICE

Two views of learning currently influence discussions of knowledge, knowing, educational practice, and educational assessment. In the first view education is defined as a process of transmitting knowledge from an expert teacher to an unsophisticated learner (Bloom, 1987; Hirsch, 1987; Rousseau, 1764/1979). Knowledge is considered external to the learner and is acquired through memorizing facts in texts, in lectures, and in the media; practicing routines and procedures developed by others; and modeling the behaviors of experts. Educators, in this view, are those who ensure that transmission is accurately delivered and received. The purpose of education is to transmit and preserve the knowledge base. The purpose of research is to systematically add to the knowledge base through rigorous and accepted procedures and through rational models that closely approximate reality.

Critics of this view hold that knowledge is not passively acquired, but is constructed by each individual through interactions with people, ideas, and environments. Knowledge is internal to the learner (Piaget, 1926; Von Glaserfeld, 1989). While knowledge growth is influenced by texts, lectures, and the media, learning occurs through dynamic interactions within a social and cultural milieu (Bakhtin, 1981; Fosnot, 1989; Vygotsky, 1962). All learning is filtered by an individual's construction based on prior learning; all constructions are affected in some way by current thoughts, feelings, and experiences. Educators, in this view, are less concerned with issues of flawless transmission and perfect reception. Instead they are concerned with helping individuals become aware of the knowledge they are continually constructing and with challenging that knowledge through discussions of alternative constructions. The purpose of education is to facilitate awareness of one's own and others' constructions. The purpose of research is to provide a steady supply of alternative ways of thinking about the universe and those who inhabit it.

Our work reflects the latter view of knowing. Our foremost concern is to explore the kinds of strategies, relationships, and contexts that facilitate knowledge construction in educational settings. Specifically, we are interested in exploring the construction of knowledge as educators inquire into their own practice and challenge or verify the meanings such practice holds for them and their students. For us, this implies that practitioners must acquire the habit of describing their current understandings, inquiring into other possible interpretations, and then reflecting upon the desirability of changing practice or maintaining the status quo. One primary influence on our thinking has been the writing of John Dewey (1933), who asserts that expertise, like knowledge, resides within the individual. Continuous learning and the steady improvement of practice depend on being open to perceiving issues and problems, and then acting in ways that will transform, clarify, and resolve issues and problems. Expertise, therefore, is not a state of being in which a researcher or a practitioner stores knowledge. Instead, expertise is a state of mind in which experience, empirical data, and knowledge of alternative solutions can blend productively to transform the status quo. As such, expertise often resides in individuals acting in specific situations. Another strong influence on our thinking came from reading the work of Donald Schön (1971, 1983), who has discussed the failure of technical expertise to solve social problems.

> Contrary to mythology, we are largely unable to 'know' in situations of social change, if the criteria of knowledge are those of the rational/experimental model. The constraints on knowing affect not only our ability to gain certainty, or probability, or precise knowledge, but our ability to establish knowledge in the rational/experimental mode at all. (Schön, 1971, p. 201)

As former classroom teachers we were accustomed to dealing with uncertainty on a daily basis. Our experiences and our reading led us to agree with Schön that all situations and all problems are open-ended—there are no definitive solutions that can be imposed from without. Each decision a participant makes is susceptible to modification or abandonment as the decision plays out in the action arena.

By formally adopting this view of knowing we university-based researchers were forced to think of research activity in a new way. We could not assume the role of educational expert, and we were not willing to create divisions between those who create knowledge and those who use knowledge. Therefore, in the design of the TFR project, the school participants had a role in naming, framing, and solving the educational problems under investigation. We agreed that for schools and universities to become places that facilitate sharing and conscious attention to knowledge construction, new relationships and roles would need to develop among school-based and university-based educators. The process did not begin as a concerted, unified effort. Indeed, if one were to interview those who worked in the early stages of the project today, they would discuss the ambiguity, uncertainty, and even hostility that occurred as new working relationships were negotiated and established (Clift, Johnson, Holland, & Veal, 1992). They would likely say that the project originally began as an innovative program in preservice teacher education. Those who joined the project later would be less likely to discuss ambiguity and more likely to assert that Time for Reflection was a self-improvement project for schools, not an extension of teacher education. We say this to foreshadow a point that we will return to in later chapters, namely, that building common agendas and common understandings is a process that may have a definable beginning, but seldom reaches a stable, or final plateau. In the next sections we describe the events that led to the development of Time for Reflection.

THE RITE BEGINNING

In 1985 the term *reflective inquiry* was incorporated into the title and the redesign of the University of Houston's undergraduate teacher preparation program, the Reflective Inquiry Teacher Education Program, or RITE. The title referred to a curriculum designed to combine field observations, course materials, and concepts across the areas of curriculum, educational psychology, school organization, sociology, and cultural studies. Renee Clift and Jane McCarthy, then assistant professors at the University of Houston, were assigned the responsibility for transforming the concept of RITE into an operational curriculum, with some support from the U. S. Department of Education, Office of Educational Research and Improvement. One component of the grant stipulated collaboration with surrounding schools. This was a welcome component, for as former public school teachers we felt that such a curriculum must include field-based teacher educators. Jane, then a school board member, was especially concerned with forming a collaboration in which teachers and principals would have a strong voice in curriculum development. The district in which she served and two other districts agreed to work closely with the university faculty responsible for moving RITE from a document to a working program.

During the summers of 1985 and 1986 teachers and principals worked with Jane, Renee, and many other University of Houston faculty members to develop a sequence of experiences that included field-based inquiry as well as practical teaching experience. One of the major strengths of the RITE curriculum was the set of projects that enabled prospective teachers to inquire into community–school relationships, district–school relationships, and teacher–student relationships. Another strength was that all education students considered what issues were common to all educators, whether their students were elementary, secondary, undergraduate, or graduate; whether the classrooms were labeled traditional academic, special subject, or special needs. Mary Lou Veal, a faculty member in physical education, continually reminded us of the importance of including all educators, not just those in academic areas, in discussions of what is best for students.

But perhaps the main strength of the RITE curriculum lay in the laboratory and classroom exercises that encouraged the prospective teachers to analyze and reflect upon the embedded values they observed in classroom practices—including their own practices prior to and during their first year of teaching. This focus on reflection and an introduction to a conception of teacher as researcher of his or her own classroom practice became the central concept for the preservice curriculum at that time. And, just as students were encouraged to study themselves, faculty began to discuss their own teaching practices and value assumptions with one another.

One of the limitations of the RITE curriculum, identified early in the implementation, was absence of time for field-based teachers to talk and reflect with the RITE students whom they supervised (Clift & Say, 1988). If practicing teachers were not able to stay after school, the only reflective conversations in which students were able to engage occurred in university classrooms. A second limitation was that the field-based teacher educators and the university-based teacher educators had no sustained time to reflect on the intended and unintended messages contained within the curriculum. Informal conversations and program evaluation questionnaires indicated a joint desire to strengthen both the program and the collaboration, but no one had any plan for how this might be accomplished.

At this time Pat Holland, a faculty member whose specialty is school supervision, joined the discussion. The conversations began to shift from a narrow focus on the reorganization of the university preservice program to a broad focus on the nature of professional relationships. Do relationships among teachers and administrators imply a quest for compliance and control through evaluation? Or do they imply support for ongoing knowledge development through conversation, negotiation, and reflection? Do current school contexts even offer a choice? And do university faculty enter into the discussion at all? As university faculty, we came to believe that we could not speak of teacher education simply in terms of the preparation of teachers, but that instead we must look at the learning opportunities for all educators, including administrators, teachers, and teacher educators.

FROM RITE TO TIME FOR REFLECTION

In 1987 university faculty submitted a proposal to the Danforth Foundation to support a network comprising university and public school participants. All of the RITE schools were invited to participate in a network designed to explore models in collaborative leadership for school-based professional development. Seven schools originally accepted the invitation. The Danforth Foundation agreed to support a planning year that was meant to provide time for reflection on the meaning of collaborative leadership. In addition, the planning year was intended to develop existing leadership skills that would make it possible for both beginning and experienced teachers to work more effectively with ethnically diverse urban communities.

By the spring of 1988, leadership teams from two senior high schools, two middle schools, and three elementary schools had agreed to participate in Time for Reflection at the same time they continued to be part of RITE. A description of these schools can be found in Figure 1.1. The three elementary schools all had female principals and were staffed predominantly by female teachers. Two of the

Figure 1.1. School Descriptions

	Location	Number of students	Number of teachers
Firestone Elementary	Near-urban	720	32
Pine Grove Elementary	Suburban	650	42
Woods Elementary	Urban	850	47
Broadstreet Middle School	Urban	2,200	110
Andrews Middle School	Urban	1,700	86
Eastview High School	Urban	2,300	95
Jefferson High School	Urban	1,600	85
Fair High School	Urban	960	51
(Joined project in second year)			

three, Firestone and Pine Grove, had worked with the RITE program from its inception. Woods joined RITE 2 years after it began. Teachers from two of the four secondary schools, Broadstreet and Jefferson, had also participated in the early design of the RITE curriculum. All four secondary schools had accepted RITE students for at least 2 years, and all had male principals when we began Time for Reflection. The principals and the teachers from these seven schools volunteered to participate in early discussions of the question, "What would it take for schools to become places where adults learn?"

For one semester teachers and principals attended a series of workshops to hear about related projects such as the Virginia Beginning Teacher Assistance Program (described in Wildman & Niles, 1987), the Mastery in Learning Project sponsored by the National Education Association (Livingston & Castle, 1989; McClure & Watts, 1990), and the Principal Leadership Program sponsored by the Danforth Foundation (Milstein, 1993). During this time the university participants tried to stress three messages: (1) we are not pushing any particular agenda, and guest speakers are invited only to provide information about similar initiatives around the country; (2) we are not in the process of developing professional development schools as envisioned by the Holmes agenda, and each school is free to develop its own project; and (3) "we have time and we have a little money, let's see what happens."

Our records at the time document that no one had any clear idea of what TFR was all about. One of the principals later wrote:

> What confused us at first was that goals for the project had not been set for us. We . . . didn't really know what we were doing for the first several meetings. Once we realized that [Time for Reflection] was what we wanted it to be—it all became clear. Then we worked on our own goals for the school.

In each school, a team comprising teachers and administrators was meeting with varying frequency, and they were all waiting for the university "experts" to tell them why. In the meantime, the university participants were waiting for the school-based "experts" to tell us what they would like Time for Reflection to mean in their schools. It seems comic now, something we laugh about when we bring the network back together to talk about our experiences and the writing of this book, but at the time it was not funny.

Establishing a Base for Decision Making

To help ourselves out of a situation in which expectations were at cross-purposes, the university team decided in the spring of 1988 that we needed to collect information—baseline data, if you will—concerning teachers' perceptions of the professional learning climate in each of the participating schools. As researchers we felt that perceptual data might help us understand each school better and might promote conversation within the teams themselves. Our reading of both John Dewey and Donald Schön helped us realize that if we labeled the problem too early, we might set off on an erroneous or even harmful solution path. All of the principals agreed that baseline data would be useful to future plans.

Research on school climate (Little, 1982; Rosenholtz, 1989), school study projects conducted by RITE students, and our own knowledge of school practice informed the development of a semi-structured interview protocol designed to inquire into the professional learning climate of each school. The interviews were designed to investigate teachers' perceptions of the school adult learning climate in general and to describe individuals' professional learning experiences in particular (for details of the entire study, see Veal, Clift, & Holland, 1989).

Three main categories described the patterns found in the interview data: school leadership, school work environment, and collaborative work patterns. Within each of these categories we found some differences in the responses of novice teachers (those with 3 or fewer years of experience) and those of experienced teachers (those with 10 or more years of experience). We will summarize the major findings within each category that are pertinent to the development of Time for Reflection.

School Leadership. We asked about the official and unofficial leaders in each school and the qualities that enabled people to lead. As one might expect, principals and assistants were often identified as the official leaders, although several interviewees expressed sentiments such as:

- A title doesn't necessarily make someone a leader.
- What do you mean by leader? Do you mean tyrant? I would call him the designated tyrant. I have yet to meet too many people here that I would classify as leaders.
- I don't see the administration as being leaders. I think they allow things to occur in various departments . . . that are just not very professional.

The novice elementary teachers and the secondary teachers we interviewed were more likely to be dissatisfied with administrative leadership than were the experienced elementary teachers. All novice teachers were more likely to mention the importance of leadership in terms of managerial skills. So were experienced secondary school teachers. Experienced elementary school teachers were more likely to mention interpersonal qualities as in the following statement: "She is very, very caring. She knows most of these children by name. She really cares. She is in the building, floating, looking, asking questions, wanting to know."

Our baseline interviews also suggested that elementary teachers had more opportunities to work in schoolwide committees than did secondary teachers. All of the interviews contained many references to the importance of positive attention and praise from administrators, and female teachers expressed this need somewhat more often than male teachers. In the three elementary schools the principals (all female) appeared to focus more on establishing and maintaining positive interpersonal relationships than did their male and secondary counterparts. The one exception to this was the Broadstreet team, who often referred to their male principal as having many of the same interpersonal qualities as the female principals.

School Work Environment. Interpersonal relationships were also mentioned as important in discussions of work environments of the schools. We found that differences among schools were often more evident than were differences related to experience or grade level. One type of interaction that appeared to cause a great deal of distress was an interaction in which teachers' work was criticized.

- I had a confrontation with a teacher who would just check up on me. She'd come over and just walk in my room, look through my lesson plans, look through my grade book, just kind of nose around my room.
- I sort of stay away from making any comment. I don't even like to observe [colleagues] because that's not in my job description. They don't appreciate it if I criticize or make a suggestion. They're just my peers.

Our data confirmed other researchers' findings that secondary teachers are more likely to affiliate with a single department than with the entire school (Bird & Little, 1985). Within the departments teachers seldom shared the same groups of students, thus inhibiting opportunities to plan together or to work toward collaborative problem solving. In addition, the secondary teachers' time after school was likely to be spent in organizing extracurricular activities. It seemed that the secondary teachers simply had less flexible time than did their elementary counterparts.

The elementary teachers in two schools worked in more open environments than in the third school, which featured self-contained classrooms. There were more reports of collegial interaction in the first two schools, due partially to the fact that children were often grouped with one teacher for math and another for reading. These teachers discussed many instances of team planning and material sharing.

Collaborative Work Patterns. As just noted, school structure seemed to have a definite effect on collaborative work patterns. Elementary teachers noted more daily communication with colleagues, but many teachers in all schools noted a desire for more communication.

- Somehow [there has to be] an easier way of problem solving as opposed to [when] you're in the bathroom and you see someone for 5 minutes and you have a problem, and you want to talk about it . . . everybody's so busy.
- There is not . . . a certain amount of time to sit down and discuss some areas which could meet a need at that point. We tend to go with the beginning and at the end, and there's a whole lot of that we could discuss in between.

In three of the secondary schools, communication between teachers and administrators was reported to be infrequent, as was ongoing communication among teachers. Our interpretation of the baseline interviews suggested that structures such as the middle school cluster meetings and the open areas in elementary schools were integral to understanding the existing norms for collaboration that existed in the schools.

Self-Selecting in . . . and out of TFR. By summer 1988, only the elementary schools and one middle school remained in the project. The two senior high schools and one middle school had withdrawn. By this time we had collected interview data from 45 secondary and 30 elementary teachers regarding their perceptions of the school environment as it affected professional learning. While we cannot be sure why the three secondary schools left the project, this baseline data provided some insight into reasons why schools may have stayed involved or chosen to detach themselves. We noted in our earliest report (Veal, Clift, & Holland, 1989) of the baseline interviews that

> To encourage teachers to discuss their learning needs and to seek help requires a supportive atmosphere that does not exist currently in many schools. . . . Modification of the status quo cannot proceed without understanding the current conditions within individual schools. This understanding must be shared among administrators and teachers, not merely evaluated by outside researchers and consultants. Our experience has shown that the development of this shared understanding requires time and a careful nurturing of work conditions including both social and professional times together. (pp. 331–332)

Of the seven schools, only Firestone Elementary School, Pine Grove Elementary School, and Broadstreet Middle School had been actively involved in the design and implementation of the RITE program. Woods Elementary School had become a RITE school during the second year of the teacher education program. Further, in the four schools remaining in TFR, teachers, not administrators, assigned RITE students to their observation teachers. Thus, participants from all four school teams had established professional working relationships with Jane, Renee, and Mary Lou prior to Time for Reflection and to any collection of baseline data. To a lesser extent this was also true of the secondary schools that left the project.

In addition to a close tie among teachers and RITE faculty, we have identified several other factors that may have influenced schools to remain involved through the early stages of ambiguity. The first, and most obvious, relates to district policy. All three of the secondary schools were in a large school district in which the superintendent had adopted a policy of transferring administrators in at least 20 buildings every 6 months. By summer 1988 all but one of the secondary school principals had been transferred elsewhere. Of those schools in which transfers occurred, only one school leadership team pressured the new principal to remain involved with Time for Reflection.

Our baseline data suggested, too, that the participants in the senior high schools had not formed collegial work habits. They were isolated in separate departments and had little or no contact with others in their buildings, particularly administrators. We stress, however, that each of the original seven schools had its own, distinct culture. While our analyses led us to search for trends and patterns across the schools, we were continually reminded that we could never think of "schools" as one.

The Network Is Established

The four schools that remained with the project did so cautiously. They knew that we had collected baseline data. They assumed that we had positive reasons for doing so and for promoting the project in general. They were even somewhat tolerant of the ambiguity surrounding Time for Reflection. But neither the remaining school teams nor the university team knew exactly how to proceed. The university participants met throughout the summer to think through our own commitment to the schools. We agreed that we were adamant about not imposing any project on the schools, but that we needed to find a way to facilitate action within and among the leadership teams. Our discussions with Bob McClure and Carol Livingston (then at NEA), Terry Wildman (working with the Virginia Beginning Teacher Assistance Program), and Donn Gresso (then at the Danforth Foundation) provided us with a practical base from which to design our own support structure. These interactions also made us aware of the intellectual debt we owed to many organizations that had wrestled with concerns similar to ours.

We began to examine consensus building activities and materials from the projects mentioned above in which external agents worked with teams from several schools to develop and implement locally designed improvement projects. These materials specified activities for developing common goals and building consensus among teams from individual schools. They also suggested multiple opportunities for participants across schools to meet together regularly to share activities, to report on progress, and to socialize with others. We began to reconceptualize Time for Reflection in terms of our roles as university facilitators. In practical terms, we began to enter a new phase of the project.

The following three questions, adapted from the NEA Mastery in Learning Project (Livingston & Castle, 1989), began a 2-day work session prior to the beginning of school.

1. What is so wonderful about your school that you would never want it to change?
2. What is so bad that it should be changed tomorrow?
3. What problems need resolutions but have no easy solutions and will require time for study?

The entire project team from two schools (Firestone and Pine Grove) attended both days; two teachers and a principal were present from Woods; and the entire Broadstreet team attended both days, but without their principal, who had been transferred from another school one month prior to the opening of school. Although she expressed support for Time for Reflection, she felt she needed to learn more about the procedures and facilities at her new school.

These workshops established the sequence of activities that would be followed at subsequent workshops: Each school's team members would share their current events and concerns. After this greeting and updating, the university team would provide a few questions for teams to discuss as a stimulus for thought and conversation about possible action. Based, in part, on the discussion, each school team would then revise or develop specific action plans, which would be shared with the entire group. At lunch, teams were encouraged to meet with members of other teams for continued sharing and conversation. After lunch, the university team and teams from other schools would provide their reflections on the action plans by raising questions about evaluation of action. The school teams would then meet in school groups to finalize plans. In between workshops, the university team met regularly to analyze progress and discuss their emerging roles in each school.

By the end of the 2-day workshop all teams had developed action plans. It seemed to us that the connection with the preservice teacher education program was becoming weaker; the local ownership of a school-based project was becoming stronger.

Moving Toward Collaboration

During the 2-day workshop, the university team debated the nature of our intervention. This debate was to continue throughout the project during the regular meetings held by the university team. We questioned what *could* be done and what *should* be done as school and university participants agreed to work with one another. Marlene Johnson, then a doctoral student, joined the university team and the debate soon after the first network meetings.

We reached early consensus on several important points. First, we agreed that our mere presence in the schools constituted intervention, and we understood that our presence would, in fact, alter what occurred while we were in the schools. Second, we agreed that the initiation of the project was a form of intervention similar to countless others in which educational researchers or experts bring a new idea into the schools for the purpose of improvement. However, we distinguished ourselves from others because we did not provide a specific direction for the schools' action plans, other than the requirement that they form collaborative teams composed of both teachers and an administrator. But beyond those two points, there was disagreement over the extent to which each individual was comfortable with interventionist activities—including the provision of workshop activities such as the ones we conducted in August 1988. We also realized that as a university team we disagreed among ourselves about how to work with schools without pre-scribing steps they should take or goals for which they might strive.

FROM ACTION RESEARCH TO ACTION SCIENCE

When Time for Reflection began we were all untenured assistant professors, with the exception of Marlene. We knew that we must publish our experiences if we wished to retain our positions in academia. Our school participants realized this too. We all understood that if we were to publish our work (and thus keep our jobs), we would need to move away from research paradigms with which we were more familiar—text analysis, comparative studies, nonparticipant observation, and quasi-experimental designs. How might we, as researchers, study our interven-tion, the professional learning cultures of the schools, and themes across schools, while at the same time continuing an intervention in an ethical, supportive, and collaborative manner? We first turned to the literature on action research for guide-lines, discussed in the following section.

A Brief Review of Action Research

The concept of action research in the United States can be traced, in part, to the work of Kurt Lewin, a social psychologist, who was concerned that research was seldom used by the very people it is often intended to inform. He proposed that studies should be grounded in the practical human problems that were en-countered on a daily basis.

> Many psychologists working today in an applied field are keenly aware of the need for close cooperation between theoretical and applied psychology. This can be ac-complished in psychology, as it has been accomplished in physics, if the theorist does not look toward applied problems with highbrow aversion or with a fear of social

problems, and if the applied psychologist realizes that there is nothing so practical as a good theory. (Lewin, 1951, p. 169)

Lewin and his students were also concerned with the relationship between autocratic leadership and group interaction as opposed to democratic leadership and group interaction. In early experimental studies of group dynamics Lewin (1948) found that there was little difference in task completion under the two leadership conditions—until the leaders left the group. Those groups that had been working with democratic leaders tended to continue working, while the other groups did not. We felt that we, as the university project directors, would need to monitor ourselves for more democratic and less autocratic leadership styles. We also felt that by monitoring ourselves we were engaging in action research on our own participation—but this did not help our school participants. Were they moving toward action research? Should we encourage them to do so?

Stephen Corey (1953) argued for action research as a way of defining relationships between classroom teachers and university professors in which the role of the university researcher would be one of consultation on problems or research questions defined by the practitioner. Corey contended that theory and practice could be linked if teachers undertook to examine practical problems of practice right in their own classrooms. The brief flurry of action research projects that resulted from Corey's ideas was short-lived in the United States, because in the 1960s educational research became linked with global events and the place of U.S. students in maintaining a competitive advantage. During the 1960s the educational research agenda was determined largely by government and private funding agencies that were under the influence of a resurgence of interest in establishing cause and effect relationships between curriculum and student outcomes. Individual teachers' priorities were deemed less important than national priorities.

Lawrence Stenhouse, in Great Britain, promoted action research by teachers as a way of improving their own classroom practice and as a method for developing hypotheses that could be tested in practice by teachers. Research, therefore, was conducted in the service of practice. Examples of this form of action research are the "Humanities Curriculum Project" and the "Ford Teaching Project" (Elliott & Adelman, 1976), which led to a series of case studies that Stenhouse believed could assist teachers in generalizing by cumulative comparison from case to case.

Although Stenhouse (1983, 1985), Rudduck (1985), Elliott (1990), and others in Great Britain continued to conduct action research projects in the 1970s and 1980s, there has been considerable pressure from other researchers and from policy makers to find generalizable links between instruction and outcomes. We would place those who seek to establish such links in our first category of researchers (parlor guests), those who believe that knowledge for teaching lies outside of the school setting. We acknowledge that many important ideas, concepts, and findings resulted from this line of educational research. It has become another useful resource for educational practitioners. We also believe that it is important for people who have the time to conduct research to do so. However, we felt that in this project the design, implementation, and evaluation of plans should reside in the local expertise of those most directly affected by the project.

We disagree strongly with the contention that the control of knowledge construction through systematic data collection and analysis belongs to "expert" educational researchers, but we also must acknowledge that many practitioners have not spent time thinking through the formation of researchable questions, nor have they thought about issues of data collection and analysis. The work of both Stenhouse and Corey has been criticized because so much emphasis was placed on teachers working as researchers. One group of critics (e.g., Hodgkinson, 1957) argued that teachers are not trained in rigorous research methods. By acting as both interventionists and data collectors, they are not able to objectively separate cause from effect.

A second line of criticism coming from both teachers and researchers is that the work of teaching is an inherently demanding job without adding one more expectation. At least one of these friendly critics (Noffke, 1992) cautions that the addition of action research as a part of teachers' expected role may overburden teachers and undermine their normal caring and concern for the children they teach. We find that we are more in sympathy with these critics than with the others, but our conception of constructivist theory, and that of reflective practice, will not permit us to simply give up on the idea of locating research within schools and classrooms as one important component of what it means to do educational research.

We find arguments concerning collaborative action research (Oja & Smullyan, 1989) quite persuasive as an answer to the critics who claim that teachers do not have the skills, training, time, or desire to carry out research. In this version of action research, those who do have the skills, training, and inclination (i.e., university researchers) carry out their studies in collaboration with teachers or administrators who have the contextual knowledge, interest, and access to student populations necessary for the purpose of answering questions that are relevant to both parties. In arguing for collaborative research, David Tripp (1989) concluded that "it is essential to find other ways of producing and institutionalizing knowledge of teaching in ways that both improve teachers' practice through their use of that knowledge, and their status through that improvement" (p. 15). When collaborative action research is designed so that the teacher is a true participant, as opposed to merely cooperating with a researcher, there is parity in the relationship as they work together toward a common goal. In this model, the university researcher often interprets the knowledge that is discovered for the teacher, so while the teacher is invested in the naming and framing of the problem, she is again excluded from the construction of professional knowledge.

Rejecting Action Research as an Intervention

The school-based participants in TFR varied with regard to their willingness to collect or analyze data. At the same time, they all agreed that the project was important to individuals and to schools, and that the relationship with the university team (as a group and as individuals) was often pleasant. They were not interested in action research; they were intrigued by the minimal intervention by the university team.

But the action research studies—even the collaborative studies—we read did not address planned interventions, or even evolutionary interventions. The term *intervention* has been used primarily in an instrumentalist sense to denote the actions of an outside agency, or change agent, on a school, often in attempts to introduce new procedures or curriculum models into the school (Berman & McLaughlin, 1978; Griffin, Lieberman, & Noto, 1983; Sussman, 1979). We referred to interventionists earlier as "interior designers." Such attempts to intervene in public school affairs often carry a serious evaluation component as researchers attempt to "prove" one curriculum, instructional method, or organizational design superior over another. Traditional approaches to intervention also imply a need to intervene because something is not working right in a school or because test scores show students are not learning. This line of thinking also takes us back to a view of research with which we were not comfortable. Such a view of intervention contradicted everything we believed about constructed knowing. Moreover, neither the university participants nor the school participants in TFR ever believed that change in school was best led by university-based researchers.

Discussions among the university participants became focused on ways we might assist in creating a collaborative professional culture wherein all participants (school and university) might work together to improve learning conditions for all students. What we could not agree upon was a way to incorporate data collection, analysis, and sharing into the process. Mentioning action research or research in general raised suspicions that the schools were only convenient sites for university participants' professional advancement. School participants' suspicions were heightened by the knowledge that while data collection and analysis were supposed to be helpful, they might actually be harmful because questions about existing school practice might be raised.

An example of this surfaced in the August 1988 work session wherein at least one principal stated that she was very displeased that the data had not yet been shared. In response, one of the university participants noted that there might be a trend in the data that suggested communication among teachers and administration might be improved at their school. The principal became somewhat defensive; the other university participants were very concerned that implications had been reported out before analysis was complete. This premature sharing carried at least three negative repercussions. The first was that school participants felt as though the data were being held privileged, which did not help build trust. The second was that the school participants felt that conclusions were reached without involving schools in the process of interpreting data. And the third was that other university team members felt that a decision to share data meant that one member was acting unilaterally, without consulting other university team members.

By the end of the first work session we realized that action research was an inappropriate strategy for our project because each school and each participant viewed action as important (although they differed with regard to the actions they valued), but that there was no similar consensus on the place of research within the project. We also realized that as a university team we had begun developing strategies for enabling action, but we had failed to develop strategies for promoting reflection. We had learned that we disagreed with one another and with our school participants on several important issues, but we had not learned how to disagree productively. As we reflected on others' action research studies and our own baseline data, we came to realize that we would need to draw from the literature called action science in order to construct our roles in the project.

A Brief Review of Action Science

> The theory of action approach begins with a conception of human beings as designers of action. To see human behavior under the aspect of action is to see it as constituted by the meanings and intentions of agents. Agents design action to achieve intended consequences, and monitor themselves to learn if their actions are effective. They make sense of their environment by constructing meanings to which they attend, and these constructions in turn guide action. In monitoring the effectiveness of action, they also monitor the suitability of the environment. (Argyris, Putnam, & Smith, 1985, pp. 80–81)

According to Argyris and Schön (1975, 1978) both individuals and organizations operate from implicit and explicit ideas about how to accomplish their goals. These ideas serve as guides that enable all humans to make sense of the everyday world as they seek to explain, predict, or control people, nature, and events. Thus we may speak of our theories of why some children learn to read before age 5; which team will win the World Series; or how to garden using environmentally safe methods of pest control. We operate theoretically in our everyday life; as educators we also operate theoretically in our work. Our theories of professional practice serve as guides for our actions in schools, classrooms, and other educational settings.

Practical theories constitute an important subcategory of theories of action, or theories of "deliberate human behavior, which is for the agent a theory of control but which attributed to the agent, also serves to explain or predict his [sic] behavior" (Argyris, Putnam, & Smith, 1985, p. 6). In other words, we act to control the education of our students by designing curricula that provide experiences that we feel are desirable means to achieving particular aims or goals. Such theories differ from their academic counterparts in that they are seldom subjected to rigorous empirical tests or to academic debates. All the same, they often guide individual decision making or institutional policy. Thus, individuals and groups may assume that a given experience or set of experiences will control learning (or at least affect it in a positive manner). Without continual examination, the validity of such assumptions may be grounded more in tradition or benign neglect as opposed to evidence of efficacy.

Argyris and Schön (1978) argue that organizations cannot learn to improve without examining tacit assumptions about organizational effectiveness. Likewise, practitioners who do not examine and reflect upon both their practice and the assumptions underlying that practice are likely to develop patterns that inhibit learning. Argyris and Schön argue further that both people and organizations develop blocking mechanisms that prevent careful scrutiny of the relations among assumptions and practice. Many times these blocks are in place accidentally; other times they are erected to protect against the discovery of error or to justify decisions. To better understand how this may work in professional education we have constructed two examples that typify practice in teacher education and administrative education.

1. The first example relates to early field experiences in teacher education. Early exposure to schools and classrooms is a routine component of most preservice teacher preparation programs. The purpose of such experiences ranges from enabling prospective teachers to develop a critical perspective on the institution of school, to allowing them to try out the role of teacher before they have invested their college career in teacher preparation, to encouraging immediate application of principles and practices taught in university-based courses. In theory, such experiences provide a foundation for continued learning. Early field experiences are presumed to shape novice teachers' thoughts and actions in pedagogically and socially acceptable ways (Zeichner, 1981). Neither policy mandates nor university syllabi are sufficient to ensure the character or quality of field work, however. Several researchers (see Zeichner, 1981) have questioned the educational value of early field experiences when those experiences reinforce racial stereotypes, promote misunderstandings about children, or inadvertently lead students to conclusions that are opposite of those envisioned by the teacher education program. In such situations experience has not proven to provide a foundation; rather it has become an obstacle to continued learning. This is not to imply that all field experiences are miseducative or a waste of time. Rather, our point here is that one cannot assume that field-based learning is, in and of itself, a positive experience for prospective teachers.

2. The second example relates to a similar, taken for granted, practice that holds

for administrative education. The term *principal as instructional leader*, which emerged from the research on effective schools, is often used to refer to an administrator's commitment to enabling learning as opposed to managing discipline within the school. Coursework in educational administration may include information about generic teaching practices derived from process–product research on teaching and coursework in supervision that focuses on conferencing with teachers about their work. These courses, which are presumed to prepare administrators to help others improve their teaching, value the actions and dispositions of individuals. In practice, however, principals' work is decoupled from teaching and learning (Hart, 1992). For professors of educational administration, therefore, an important issue is whether the professional preparation is appropriate for the work conditions of practice. It is conceivable that a focus on the individual administrator in relation to individual teachers does not enable one to encourage leadership throughout the school. Rather, principals may need to reorganize the social and professional learning context so that teachers might learn from one another. As with preservice teacher education, one cannot simply assume that time-honored course requirements are satisfactory in and of themselves.

To investigate the efficacy of a given educational practice in all schools and universities it is important to examine what the practitioners *hope* will happen (the stated goals or explicit values); to examine what processes are thought to be in place that are designed to bring about these stated goals or exemplify desired values; and then to examine what processes are operating that either do or do not enable the desired ends. Ideally, this would be accomplished by people within an organization, but this is difficult because there may be a conflict of interest as an insider uncovers information that may be damaging to others. It is also possible that organizations (particularly schools) cannot afford to train or to employ people whose only job is to question and investigate current practice. Researchers, whether they employ quantitative or qualitative methods, are trained to criticize and question the status quo. Organizational consultants can also serve as questioners. Since researchers and consultants are both external to the situation, there is a strong possibility that they do not have a vested interest in maintaining the status quo or in protecting a particular individual, group, or practice.

In their book *Action Science*, Argyris, Putnam, and Smith (1985) suggest that an external consultant (and we would add, researcher) can determine the stated goals and values by examining specific written and oral statements from individuals and from documents produced by the organization. These are labeled *espoused theories*, or theories of what controls are in place that produce desirable outcomes or inculcate desirable values. These espoused theories can then be compared with the processes a school, university, or other organization employs as it goes about routine operations. Because conceptions of value and efficacy are expressed by actions as well as words, they can constitute *theories in action*, or controls that are in place that send out messages congruent with or incongruent with the espoused theories. Actions have the potential to send clearer and stronger messages than espoused theories, since, by their nature, they have a more immediate impact on people than do slogans, mission statements, or statements of what is desirable.

For example, a school district or a principal may state that continued professional development is important for all school staff because it will increase learning opportunities for students. This espoused theory may be followed by a confirming theory in action when the principal provides information about professional development activities and also provides as much funding for such activities as she can possibly arrange. This action sends a message that the principal means what she says. However, her theory in action may negate or conflict with her espoused theory if she inadvertently withholds information from her staff members or refuses to permit them to attend professional activities during school hours.

Argyris, Putnam, and Smith (1985) argue persuasively that it is often difficult for people inside an organization to identify and reflect upon gaps between those theories they identify as important and their subsequent actions. While this may occur for many reasons, we will discuss only three that seem especially relevant to schools. The first, most obvious reason is that teachers and principals have enough to do without collecting and analyzing data. Time is a scarce resource, and decisions about time allocation understandably favor contact with students. The second is that most organizations have formed operating norms that emphasize celebration of success, not the documentation of failures. Schools are certainly no exception to this norm. Problems are frequently seen as signs that someone or some group has failed, as opposed to naturally occurring events in any social structure. Finally, people within organizations are often prepared to perform a specific set of tasks, which do not include the collection and analysis of data about the functions of the organization itself. Teacher preparation and administrator preparation may include experiences in working with data on student achievement and attitudes, evaluation of teacher behavior, or even school finance. But the application of these skills is seldom, if ever, exercised to systematically study the holistic organization and functions of the school.

Time for Reflection as Action Science

The five co-authors, who were trained as traditional researchers with backgrounds in both quantitative and qualitative methodologies, did not begin the project with a view of becoming action scientists. And, we hasten to add, we were not trained by Chris Argyris or his colleagues. We were familiar, however, with action research and with Argyris and Schön's (1978) work on learning in organizational settings, particularly their argument that action implies theory. In Time for Reflection, leadership teams began by thinking about the unique characteristics of their schools and about what changes they thought would be of benefit to their students and colleagues. With our reading of action science we felt that we had found a methodological tool that would allow us to facilitate the interventions that the school participants desired and that would enable us to study our mutual endeavors collaboratively. Finally, in action science we found a theoretical framework that matched our desire to create time for reflection among a group of educators. Argyris, Putnam, and Smith (1985) define action science as "working with a community to create conditions in which members can engage in public reflection on substantive matters of concern to them and also on the rules and norms of inquiry they customarily enact" (p. 34). With this form of intervention, the members of the university team felt comfortable in moving forward.

SUMMARY

Time for Reflection began as an outgrowth of a collaborative school–university teacher education program, but rapidly evolved into a rather complex project in collaborative leadership and school-based project management. The university team (and co-authors) planned, argued, and negotiated methods for working with the school-based teams comprising administrators and teachers. The administrators and teachers began planning, arguing, and negotiating desired changes in their respective schools. All participants planned, argued, and negotiated appropriate contributions to individuals, schools, and the project as a whole.

Thus, within the context of the project we found it necessary to become comfortable with many concepts that we had not previously examined or questioned in relation to school–university collaboration. For the co-authors the most difficult concepts to redefine included *reflection, intervention, research*, and *collaboration*. In Chapter 2 we discuss our current understanding of these concepts, an understanding based on what we have come to label as *professional reflective activity*.

Professional Reflective Activity: Definitions and Processes

> The function of reflective thought is . . . to transform a situation in which there is experienced obscurity, doubt, conflict, disturbance of some sort, into a situation that is clear, coherent, settled, harmonious. (Dewey, 1933, pp. 100–101)

> As the professional moves toward new competencies, he gives up some familiar sources of satisfaction and opens himself to new ones. He gives up the rewards of unquestioned authority, the freedom to practice without challenge to his competence, the comfort of relative invulnerability, the gratification of deference. (Schön, 1983, p. 299)

The Dewey quote, here taken out of the context of an entire book, suggests that the outcome of reflective thought is harmony. The Schön quote, also taken out of context, suggests that the outcome of reflective practice is uncertainty. In our view, both are correct because we view reflection in teaching and professional education as a continuous process. At any particular time one may experience confusion or disturbance. To work through this period—alone or with colleagues—educators may analyze the problem, pose alternative solutions, and then embark on a series of actions that lead to a tentative resolution. At any particular time educators may experience the dissipation of a tentative resolution. Knowing this can lead educators to both expect the unexpected and to search for hidden flaws within all plans before, during, and after implementation.

Subsequent to Schön's work and the renewed interest in Dewey's earlier writings, many authors have commented on the multiple meanings people bring to the word *reflection* (Clift, Houston, & Pugach, 1990). We came to prefer the phrase *professional reflective activity* because we view reflection as an ongoing process, not a product or an outcome. Depending on the issues or topics to be addressed, the immediate context in which reflection occurs, and the available data, the nature of reflection can take several different forms. Thus, the term *reflection* in the title of our project conveys the notion of reflection as an activity, as well as a process. In such activities professional educators have opportunities to revisit, review, and reanalyze their work. We would like to emphasize here that what we are talking about is not a single event. Rather we envision many planned (as well as spontaneous) occasions in which educators come together to assess the meaning, value, and effects of current practice. In this chapter we first elaborate on our definitions of reflection using examples from the project as illustrations. We then discuss the contextual dimensions that we found affect ongoing professional reflectivity. In the final section we elaborate on the relationships that emerged to support reflection, action, and research.

PROFESSIONAL REFLECTIVE ACTIVITY
AND EDUCATIONAL PRACTICE

In our reading we found four categories of reflective activity to be especially relevant to our project.

1. Technical analysis of action in relation to educational research
2. Personal analysis of one's own development as an educator
3. Critical analysis of the implicit and explicit values embedded in educational settings and activities
4. Communal analysis of individual interpretations of experience

We would like to emphasize that we found all of these forms to be valuable assets in the project. We do not wish to imply that one form is more valuable than another, but we do feel that it is unwise for educators to limit professional discussions to only one form. As with most social science category systems, the boundaries among the four are not clear. And, we add, different individuals may label the same situation or scenario differently, based on their background and current world view. Celebrating such ambiguity and diversity is an important part of what it means to have a reflective conversation. In the following sections each definition is preceded by an example taken from our fieldnotes and cross-checked with school and university participants for accuracy. While we have not done so, it would be an interesting exercise to discuss each scenario by using several alternative forms of reflection.

Technical Analysis of Action

Susie, in her first month as an elementary physical education teacher, is concerned about accommodating her teaching to the lesson cycle that is encouraged through the use of the Texas Teacher Appraisal System (TTAS). The TTAS is a state-mandated, low inference observation system designed to evaluate novice and experienced teachers in all subject areas and at all grade levels. If Susie receives a low rating, she will be delayed in reaching the next level of the career ladder, which means that she will not receive the salary stipend that accompanies promotion. If her ratings are very low, she can be placed on probation and fired if there is no improvement. Susie discusses her interpretation of how the TTAS applies to physical education with Mary Lou, one of her former professors: "To me there are some problems with my philosophy of how [physical education] should be versus my trying to have a good evaluation." Mary Lou listens to Susie describe her struggle to demonstrate the verbal teacher input required for a good evaluation balanced against her feeling that she should talk less and have her students do more physical activity. . . . "I know how to put on a good lesson like a classroom teacher, but I just don't think it's appropriate [the verbal input] every day." Together they discuss how some aspects of the TTAS accommodate to physical education more than others.

Technical reflection involves checking one's instruction for fidelity or accuracy as it relates to research on teaching effectiveness. In Texas, administrative policy, as well as the construction of the TTAS, was based on the presumption of scientific evidence that could prescribe desirable teaching practice. But this is not the only form of technical reflection. It can also involve reviewing children's answers to questions in order to determine potential misunderstandings or errors in their thinking. Susie's example was very common in all of the schools. Many times a teacher would become concerned that his or her performance was not consistent with those aspects of teaching measured by the state appraisal process. Our fieldnotes document numerous conversations in which teachers expressed their concerns to us, to administrators, and to one another. In several instances teachers asked us to observe them and even videotape them so that they might better reflect on their teaching practice.

Within the school districts, attention also turned to a body of research that has identified school-level variables that correlate with improved test scores (Edmonds, 1979; Good & Brophy, 1986). In many districts administrators are still being encouraged to change their practices to implement these correlates of effective schooling in their buildings. One of our participating principals was regularly asked to share her knowledge of the correlates with districts surrounding the greater Houston area. As principals, superintendents, and other administrators think through their practices in relation to the body of research often labeled effective schooling or effective teaching, they too are engaging in technical reflection.

Van Manen (1977) has elaborated on this concept of technical reflection, tracing its development back to David Hume and others who represent an empirical-analytic epistemology. We agree with his argument that current practitioners who embrace this tradition assume that the teacher (and the principal)

> must learn to apply a variety of techniques to the curriculum and to the teaching-learning process so that a predetermined set of objectives can be realized most efficiently and most effectively. . . . The dominant position of empirical-analytic science in education and curriculum assures that the practical question is converted almost automatically into an instrumental one: How can knowledge make the curriculum more effective, more efficient, and more productive? The point is not that these are bad questions, but that there are other questions to be asked. (p. 210)

Technical knowledge is only one source of information used by thoughtful practitioners. If we slightly modify the example provided at the beginning of this section, so that the teacher is not the focus of our example, it is easy to see why knowledge gleaned from research is an important contributor to practice, but cannot automatically prescribe practice. Suppose a prospective teacher, upon viewing a tape of her teaching, notices that one child has been inattentive during the entire class period. This simple change raises a number of complicated questions regarding how one might interpret this phenomenon. Should she label the child as uncooperative? sleepy? bored? stupid? gifted? Should she place responsibility for the inattention on the temperature of the room? the child's home environment? her lesson? the curriculum? What steps should she take next? assign a detention? call home? talk with the child individually? talk with another teacher? ignore the situation? At present we do not have an empirical data base from which we might advise her—although many of us have had experiences very similar to hers.

The way our hypothetical novice teacher interprets the situation and the actions she takes are dependent on many factors. Some are related to her professional education (Grossman & Richert, 1988), some to her level of expertise (Carter, Cushing, Sabers, Stein, & Berliner, 1988), and some to the school culture in which she works (Rosenholtz, 1989). Teaching and administration are both practical activities conducted in complex environments. We found that appeals to technical knowledge moved professional reflective discussions from relying solely on experience to critical analyses of claims and counterclaims by researchers and by practitioners. As with most everything else in this project, there was considerable diversity in the groups as to the values they placed on technical knowledge. There was also considerable diversity in the way people responded during such discussions. Professional reflective activity involves access to as many knowledge bases as possible, but it also involves dynamic interactions among the discussants. As such, it is our opinion that conceptions of professional interactions cannot (and should not) be separated from who we are as people.

Reflective Analysis of Personal Development

Arthur, the team leader, was acutely aware of the strong personalities who constituted the Broadstreet leadership team. He once remarked that he was "riding herd on a team of broncos." In several telephone conversations with university team members he expressed concern that the team might disband because of interpersonal friction among members. Several times he thought about resigning himself, for he had joined the team to work with a tutorial program for students—not to mediate among adults. Still, he persisted even though he could not articulate why.

He used conversations with the university facilitators to discuss his doubts, challenges, and triumphs. On one such occasion he was discussing a incident in which he had persuaded two key members to remain on the team by talking individually with each one. As he related his evolving conception of self as teacher leader, we asked how he had worked through this incident. He replied that he had listened carefully to each one and re-alized that both members were important to the success of the team's many projects. "I told them that we needed them both." He often referred to this incident as a personal triumph.

Personal reflection, as it played out in our work, often concerned relation-ships with students, local colleagues, and state and national colleagues, and the ongoing development of those relationships. In conversations prior to and subse-quent to the example, Arthur often wondered why he had been elected team leader. He also wondered how he might mend rifts that developed as people on his team disagreed with one another—and whether he had any right to call university team members at home to discuss his doubts. Arthur's role was changing in that he was becoming concerned with developing and maintaining a project that affected the entire school. Unlike the previous example, there was no readily available research base to which Arthur felt he could appeal for guidance. His reflections on learn-ing to be the team leader were clearly not technical. Rather, they were *personal* in that Arthur often talked about his goals, his feelings, and his experiences as they related to others on his team and to the university team. They were also *practical* in that they focused on what actions he might take or had taken.

The work of Michael Connelly, Jean Clandinin, and Freema Elbaz has de-fined and elaborated the construct of personal practical knowledge through case studies of administrators and teachers. Elbaz's (1983) case study of Sarah, a high school English teacher, was the basis for her theory that personal practical knowl-edge is influenced by an individual's image of self and of self as teacher. An image guides judgment, analysis, and planning, but it is not situation specific.

Drawing on Elbaz's theory, Clandinin's (1985) work with Stephanie, an ele-mentary school teacher, described the ways in which Stephanie's image of class-

room as "home" served as a guide for her curriculum planning as well as her interactions with students. In related work, Connelly's (Connelly & Clandinin, 1988)
interviews with Phil, an elementary school principal, document the ways his early
life experiences affected his current interactions with the school community—
including his interactions with parents. It is important to note here that image is
not always consciously articulated. In all three studies mentioned above, the
research process itself stimulated an awareness and identification of the relationships between the personal and practical as they impact on professional development.

Throughout Time for Reflection we found that we could not ignore the occasions in which all participants, not excluding ourselves, spent considerable time
and energy wondering if participation was consistent with our personal constructs
of self as educator. We briefly referred to one example at the end of Chapter 1. As
we moved toward an action science perspective, we felt that our images of self as
researcher were being challenged. Learning how to work together often left us in
doubt as to whether we should, indeed, work together. Working with others in
collaborative relationships stimulates considerable personal reflection as well as
professional reflection. We found examples of this in team teaching situations, in
leadership team analyses, and in numerous conversations among members of the
university-based project team. Many of the heated discussions concerned the process of negotiating projects that brought questions of value into play. In ongoing
reflective discussions of school projects, we found that participants often questioned the relative worth of one project versus another. Moreover, when such discussions and projects were examined more closely, we found that we were unaware, at the time, of those values we demonstrated through both words and actions.

Critical Analysis of the Implicit and Explicit Values

When Marlene joined Time for Reflection she agreed to work with the two
other graduate students to conduct interviews with novice and experienced
teachers. She also knew that she would be assisting Renee with RITE and
would also work with the logistics of the project, carrying out tasks the
faculty preferred not to work on themselves. Although she was asked for
substantive advice and input, she and two other graduate students (who
were not paid for their work on the project) demurred from contributing a
strong voice. Privately they agreed that collaborative leadership was a
concept that did not apply to graduate assistants.

When Marlene decided to continue with the project in the second
year, she challenged the previously unquestioned assumption that graduate
students should serve primarily as faculty assistants. As responsibilities
were negotiated for the coming year, she strongly stated that if she was
expected to engage in project activities, she should have an equal voice in

all decisions related to the project. At this point it became very clear to the faculty participants that they had inadvertently created a hierarchy contradicting the values they espoused in their work with school colleagues.

This led to a renegotiation of project responsibilities within the university team. But it led to much more. Prior to this point the focus of many of our conversations had been directed outward, toward the schools. Now we realized that many of the issues of collaboration, leadership, and interpersonal relations we observed as a part of our research were closer than we had allowed ourselves to realize before Marlene's challenges.

Van Manen (1977) draws from Habermas's articulation of critical insight into power relationships among individuals in what he terms the highest level of reflection implying "a commitment to an unlimited inquiry, a constant critique, and a fundamental self-criticism" (p. 221). Early in the project the university team interpreted this to mean a conscious attempt to think about why certain norms, patterns, and routines exist and the relationship between those routines and the social, moral, and ethical impact on children and others who inhabit schools. We came to realize that we must study and analyze our own behaviors, including the norms, patterns, and routines that we perpetuate through interactions among our immediate research team as well as those across teams. This is difficult to do unless concerns are voiced for open discussion.

Within Time for Reflection, the difficulty became acute discomfort when participants began to share negative information. Negative information was anything that was important to any of the school or university projects that was not positive or encouraging. All participants were afraid of hurting someone's feelings, of putting themselves in a dangerous political situation, or of seeming to be cynical, judgmental pessimists. Still, in attempting to form collaborative relationships to make changes in ourselves and to engage in professional reflective activity that actively critiqued plans, processes, and outcomes, we could not blind ourselves to the value dimensions of what we said we valued and what we expressed through action and through language. The university-based participants were often concerned that we were sending messages that university-interpreted, data-based knowledge should supplant that of practitioner-interpreted, experience-based knowledge. We still are not sure that we are emotionally ready to accept negative information that conflicts with our images of ourselves.

In the previous section we noted the possibility that working in a group can promote conscious attention to reflection on self as person. We add that working in a group struggling to become, at once, consciously reflective and collaborative can promote critical attention to the value dimensions of our work and the power dimensions of our relationships. Central to both of these is the idea of educators coming together to form a community in which critical analysis is celebrated, but individuals as persons are not denigrated. With that in mind we turn to the fourth aspect of reflection that we encountered in our work.

Communal Analysis Synthesizing Individual Interpretations

Each school in Suburban Independent School District has established a team of teachers and counselors who meet with teachers, parents, and often both to review a particular student's progress, to brainstorm ways of assisting the student, and to offer advice and support to both parents and teachers. These CORE teams meet before and after school. Any teacher or parent can request to be on the agenda.

On this particular afternoon Laura, a third-grade teacher, was discussing a child who, "When I ask him questions, he doesn't seem to understand me." Other teachers began to offer information and ideas regarding this phenomenon. Each suggestion was discussed while the counselor took notes in preparation for a meeting with the child's mother. After the discussion, Laura and the counselor summarized the next steps Laura would take.

Jeffrey Cinamond and Nancy Zimpher (1990), drawing on the work of Herbert Mead and John Dewey, distinguish between the conception of a reflective individual and reflection as a function of community. In their view, educational settings are enhanced as people move from isolated experiences in their own classrooms or offices toward communities in which experience serves as a basis for discussions of practice, theory, and educational values. Experience, therefore, becomes reconstructed and reinterpreted over time as a function of both time and communal negotiation and interpretation.

In the example a teacher had identified something about a student that was troubling her and looked to her colleagues for help. The teachers at her school had a history of working together on many projects. Therefore, the CORE team was viewed by these teachers as an extension of previous efforts. They felt comfortable talking with one another about issues related to students.

Within the project Time for Reflection there was some shared history of working together within the context of RITE. It is our opinion that the years spent with RITE made it possible to envision a community of educators in several buildings who felt comfortable talking and reflecting with one another. Moving from the concept to the reality, however, is more complex than calling a meeting or discussing a plan. At the same time, studying the process in order to learn from it is more complex than collecting data and subjecting them to qualitative analysis. Within the community, we were developing a conception of experience in which the meaning of a given event was (and is) not stable. In other words, in reflecting on our work we find that we have reconstructed the meanings of events over the years.

Another example of how one group's interpretation of an event's meaning may change over time is found in Lanzara's (1991) account of a university-based faculty group engaging in a professional development project related to the design and adoption of a computer music system. Lanzara utilized a research method in which he became a participant observer in faculty seminars, taking notes on conversations and debates. From these data he inferred themes that were relevant to the instructional design process. As is customary in such research, he then returned to share his interpretations with the participants. In his account of this process he noted that different participants held varying perspectives on the process, which often differed from his interpretation. This did not surprise him. What was troubling was his sense that the same participants shifted their interpretations of the events from their initial discussions. Lanzara accounted for this by arguing that the original accounts or interpretations enable one to make sense of complex situations, but these are discarded as those situations evolve over time. An event, therefore, "is *extended* into an ever evolving sequence of descriptions" (p. 308, emphasis in original).

As we worked through the development, implementation, and analysis of Time for Reflection, we also found that meanings and interpretations changed over time. New experiences, professional readings, formal feedback sessions, informal conversations, and the process of writing have all shaped and reshaped our individual memories of the project, as well as our current understandings of the implications for ourselves and our colleagues. The fact that we have data, both the original fieldnotes and our individual and negotiated analyses of those fieldnotes, allows us to trace the evolution of our thinking. Our discussion of Time for Reflection is based on those qualitative data collected systematically over a 3-year period, but our discussions while writing this text also serve as a reflective reconstruction of our experiences. Once we met weekly, or daily if necessary, to talk through Time for Reflection, but we now "talk" via electronic mail, make hour-long telephone calls, and meet infrequently at national conferences. Professional reflective activity involves more than attention to multiple forms of reflection. We found (and still find) that context can either facilitate or destroy opportunities for individuals to reflect on practice or for education participants to form communities in which they may reflect with one another.

DIMENSIONS INFLUENCING EDUCATORS' OPPORTUNITIES TO REFLECT

We first identified contextual dimensions affecting professional reflective activity based on data from the original seven participating schools. Four original schools plus one new high school stayed with the project until it ended. We then refined and used the dimensions as one way to sort our observations and interviews with the five schools that worked together throughout the project (Clift, Holland, & Veal, 1990; Clift, Veal, Johnson, & Holland, 1990). Since our original analysis we have become aware of others' attempts to develop similar categories (Johnson, 1993a; Peters &Waterman, 1982), as others who are involved in more conventional studies also attend to the interaction among context and professional development.

Structural Dimension

This dimension refers to time and to space. Finding space for adults to meet and talk with one another freely without interruption was a problem in all but one of the schools. In Woods Elementary School, for example, five leadership team members and three university team members crowded into the tiny, windowless counselor's office for an hour-long meeting. Other times we met after school and sat in chairs designed for young children. In other schools talk occurred in hushed voices as we met in libraries so that we would not entirely disturb those students and teachers who were also using the library facilities.

Overcrowding in the schools made the issue of space very difficult to resolve, although the need for adult space away from students was widely recognized. The absence of defined physical spaces in schools where teachers, administrators, visitors, parents, and any combination of the four can meet and work together sends an implicit message that such meetings are not valued. This situation diminishes the importance of such meetings and the opportunities for collaborative work or professional reflective activity. For Broadstreet Middle School, the issue of space for adults became an important part of the action plans—the leadership team arranged for an equipment storage room to be converted to a work space and meeting space for teachers.

Resolving the issue of physical space is relatively easy compared with the issue of time in which to meet together. In all of the schools teachers were busy with other commitments before and after school; team members did not share a common lunch half-hour; and there were no permanent substitutes or aides to help cover classes. Within a particular grade or level some teachers met together while their students worked with special-subject teachers in art or physical education. Many times issues were deferred and discussions were left unfinished because the students had to be picked up from their special class. Only in Broadstreet Middle School, where the teachers were clustered into teams that had common times for meeting together, did we observe a conscious attempt to modify time so that teachers might meet and work together.

As we can attest from trying to write while co-authors are in different states, it is much easier to engage in forms of professional activity when your colleagues are close and when time is dedicated to such discussions. When we began to think about helping people find time and space to work together, we realized that this would be a mainstay of our intervention. We also realized that we, as a university team, would have to place a priority on allocating time to meet together as well as time to meet with our school colleagues. We noted (wryly) that university professors, whose spaces are designed for adults to meet and whose time is extremely flexible, seldom engage in professional reflective activity on teaching with colleagues. Time and space are necessary, but are insufficient.

Individual Dimension

Working with other professionals successfully and building a reflective community of educators depends, in part, on how individuals are encouraged to participate in the discussion. Within each of our schools we observed that some teachers and administrators had strong, positive feelings about collaborating with colleagues, with administrators, and with university faculty. We also saw that a number of individuals preferred to be left alone. This by itself is not surprising since we would expect to see individual differences in any organization. We realized, however, that individual differences could not be ignored. All participants noted the importance of being sensitive to individuals as well as to the differences in professional learning needs that occur as a function of teaching experience, school context, and curriculum. Within our data we identified several individuals who felt threatened by or distanced from a particular activity or project. We also identified people who valued action, but who thought time spent analyzing and discussing was wasted effort. Equally important, but less obvious, were instances where individual desires or needs were in conflict with those of the group. We observed this in the schools and we experienced it ourselves.

Earlier we agreed with Schön that an individual who is a reflective professional must tolerate a high degree of ambiguity and uncertainty. We now add that building reflective communities requires additional sensitivity to the dynamic relationships between the individual and the group. While conflict is both healthy and inevitable, resolving such conflict is difficult and not always possible.

Interpersonal Relationships

Our early interviews and subsequent fieldwork confirmed and reconfirmed that creating and maintaining relationships with colleagues were very important to our school participants. They are also important to the co-authors. In schools, the factors we identified as important influences on these relationships included formal social interactions among school staff, overt and covert messages that contributions to the school are valued, and opportunities to participate in informal conversations and occasions in which praise or criticism is shared. Learning to disagree and remain friends was a goal of all participants. While it may be important to surface negative information, it was much more important to maintain positive professional and personal relationships with the teacher across the hall and the team member working on the Time for Reflection project.

Our data included numerous examples of interactions in which people were told they were not doing enough, they had transgressed, or they were expendable. Opportunities for celebration and public messages that recognize positive educational contributions were very scarce. As a dimension, interpersonal relations can support and encourage confidence in one's skills, create opportunities to take risks and make mistakes, and provide a context for developing new perspectives on teaching, learning, and schooling. We realized that all participants (including ourselves) might focus so closely on what we had not accomplished at any point in time that we might forget to recognize what we had accomplished. In reflecting on action it is important to celebrate those actions that worked out well.

Leadership

Analysis of the baseline interviews suggested that virtually all of the teachers identified the principal or another administrator as the official leader of the school, but their descriptions and evaluations of administrators varied considerably from school to school. These teachers often stated that they expected administrators to manage the daily building routines competently, plus provide support for teachers. A principal's support, therefore, often meant keeping discipline under control and providing reassurance that teachers were competent and valued. Our data also contained references to others in the building—assistant principals, teachers, and librarians—who acted in leadership capacities. This led us to think in terms of leadership roles within the project as opposed to defining leadership in terms of one person. It also led us to think very carefully about the leadership roles we did and did not occupy in our intervention into the schools' lives.

Our working view of leadership was never synonymous with the terms *principal*, *administrator*, or *professor*. When there is collaboration across institutions and across role groups, we expected that there would be considerable ambiguity regarding who is responsible for what actions. As we have reported elsewhere (Clift, Johnson, Holland, & Veal, 1992), the school participants gradually also came to consensus that this ambiguity was desirable. Still, we cannot deny the importance of overt support and commitment from the person who is the designated building leader and the designated district leader. A designated leader who is willing to let others lead as well is more likely to establish a climate in which educators feel that rewards and risks are shared among reflective professionals.

Synergy

As you might expect, our analysis of the data suggested to us that the four previously mentioned dimensions overlap considerably. This led us to speculate that the degree to which all of the dimensions worked together could either build on each other to create a highly positive learning climate, or conflict with one another to create an atmosphere that was hostile to professional learning. In becoming more and more involved in work across institutions to create conditions that would maximize the professional learning climate, we began to see the university role as helping teachers and administrators subtly reshape business as usual.

Within the entire project our conception of synergy necessarily included the contribution of university educators to the professional learning culture within schools. Perceptions of the importance of our presence and of our absence affected school participants' willingness to work with us and, to a certain extent, with one another. The school participants had committed to doing something—and we had committed to helping them do whatever they specified in their action plans. At times, this "help" meant reminding school participants that, although we realized school problems might occasionally prevent attention to the project, we did expect that the teams would follow through on their commitments. At other times the school participants reminded us that "help" meant more than taking fieldnotes and analyzing data. Together, as a total group of participants, we were beginning to fashion relationships that were somewhat different from our earlier work together for supporting preservice teacher education, and somewhat different from the ways university-based researchers had worked cooperatively with school-based practitioners in the past.

NEW RELATIONSHIPS AND SUPPORTIVE INTERVENTION

The school participants' expectations of us raised important questions about how we might sustain a community in which ideas about teaching and learning might be shared and debated. In this section, we describe what we term *supportive intervention* as it evolved over time and within the collaborative network we all (school and university participants) came to value and depend on. The university team members realized early in the project that it was impossible to make universal predictions or prescriptions for the schools. Rather, we had to remain grounded within the situations as we found them and with events as they happened. As we did so, we found that we grew in our appreciation of what was healthy and good about each school and in our ability to appreciate their existing cultures. While as interventionists, even supportive ones, we earnestly hoped for positive outcomes from our efforts, we recognized how important it was for us to refrain from any attempts to dictate our ideas about what should happen in each school.

This meant, in some cases, an agonizingly slow process of learning to trust one another. How well we remember the frequently repeated question from members of the leadership teams during the first year of the project: "What do you want us to do?" We, and they, often felt frustrated with the consistent answer, "What do *you* want to do?" When we began meeting together, we rather naively assumed that bringing school participants together and providing a context for thoughtful discussion would automatically spark a discussion of school problems.

Within organizations the culture often operates to suppress identifying and discussing problems. Instead organization members often adopt a facade of a politeness in order to minimize conflict. In schools another cultural factor is operating in that individual teachers stay away from discussions involving conflicting views and opinions because they wish to focus solely on the needs of students in their individual classrooms. It takes time to envision the possibility that reflecting together may facilitate action in the classroom.

Supportive intervention, therefore, came to mean the understandings about communal reflection as we developed into a community of educators participating in an open-ended process that incorporated action and reflection on action. Within our young community we all learned to tolerate a high degree of ambiguity as individual school teams worked through their own process of developing action plans specific to their unique cultures and needs. We learned that we must reflect *with* one another as opposed to reflecting *on* the actions of others.

Interventions by the University Team

After the initial summer workshop described in Chapter 1, the university team began to organize working with individual school team members. Our first decision was to have one university team member serve as a primary contact person for each team, with a second team member working as a not so silent partner. Our second decision was to keep records of all contacts with schools and school participants and to share detailed summaries of these contacts with one another for discussion. Our third decision was to share our interpretations of the fieldnotes with the team. Our final decision was to carefully record any direct intervention we made in the life of the school, no matter what the connection to TFR. As we analyzed our fieldnotes, we sorted our interventions into the following categories: (1) creating time for planning, sharing, and communal reflecting; (2) regular site visits and helping with school-specific requests; and (3) providing data-based feedback.

Creating Time for Planning, Sharing, and Communal Reflecting. An important feature of the project was the provision of release time to leadership team members to work on project-related activities. Danforth funding provided for a minimum of 5 days of substitute moneys for each teacher each semester. The participating school districts agreed to match funds for substitute teachers to cover team members' attendance at network meetings, absences from the building for the purpose of data collection, and participation in project-related activities within the building.

From the beginning to the end of the project, time, as it is currently structured in schools, was cited as a major deterrent to the ability of school teams to plan, implement, and evaluate their projects. In addition to providing funding for substitutes, we also assigned student teachers to work with team members in all five project schools. Our (and the school participants') intention was that when these student teachers proved capable of working alone in the classroom, the teachers would have a few hours each week to work on project-related activities. This version of differentiated staffing proved effective in two of the elementary schools, where teachers were able to work out release time for some teachers within a grade-level pod by sharing the supervision of student teachers. In the remaining three schools, where classrooms were isolated structurally from each other, members of the leadership team were not able to arrange release time while student teachers were present. Having student teachers also did not help to provide release time in schools when principals did not assign student teachers to team members, when principals did not explicitly encourage in-school meetings, or when a student teacher needed extremely close supervision by the university and the cooperating teacher.

The university team attempted several times to gently push school team members into buying time by using project money to arrange for substitute teachers. In several cases, teachers expressed some concern about leaving their classes, and felt that preparing for substitutes was somewhat burdensome. In one school teachers actively resisted the idea of meeting during school time and were perfectly willing to meet after school or at night. The remaining four schools used release time to attend network meetings and statewide conferences, observe one another's classes, plan for local project-related activities, visit other schools in the project, and evaluate project activities.

In addition to encouraging teams to meet together on their own campuses, the university team organized biannual, day-long network meetings. The leadership teams met together a total of seven times during the 3-year project. These meetings were originally conceptualized as serving two primary purposes: (1) to provide the leadership teams with staff development necessary for them to enhance their collaborative skills and their knowledge of teachers' professional development needs; and (2) to provide the teams with time to develop their action plans and then, later, to evaluate their progress and to modify action plans as necessary. They also served as occasions for all of us to share perceptions of the entire project's progress. Although bringing all the teams together at the network meetings was intended to serve an additional purpose of providing them with an opportunity to share ideas and experiences, such sharing was not intended to be a major focus of the meetings. For the leadership teams, however, the scheduled "brag sessions," in which teams reported on their plans and accomplishments, became a highlight. These sessions also became more elaborate as time went on, as these examples from our fieldnotes illustrate.

The Broadstreet team arrived last and they entered the room in unison, wearing matching T-shirts bearing the school name and mascot. Their unity as a team was established as Arthur, their leader, announced that "staying together is our biggest accomplishment." The team proceeded to enumerate a long list of additional accomplishments. The handout that accompanied the team's presentation had a heading that read "We are buzzing with excitement."

The Woods team came to the network meeting armed with a poster illustrating all of the ways they collaborate. The entire team, including the principal, stood together in front of us to explain their view of collaboration. Hand prints encircled the poster, demonstrating how each person makes a special and important contribution to the team's projects. Their presentation highlighted their recognition that better communication was needed in the building, but it also illustrated the extent of their accomplishments since the beginning of the project.

One other important aspect of the network meetings was the contribution good food made to the leadership team members' sense of the meetings as special events. While the provision of food may sound inconsequential, the meals served as a symbolic gesture that their presence was valued, and many leadership team members commented about how much they appreciated the delicious lunches served at the network meetings. The social interactions that occurred during those special lunches were vital to the development of trust and mutual respect. At the same time they provided a time of mutual recommitment to a shared purpose.

Network meetings demonstrated the reflective aspect of constructed knowing since they provided occasions for collective thinking about the schools' projects and about the larger issues of professional culture and collaboration. They also demonstrated the use of reflection both as a response to and a source of participants' continually changing understanding of those projects. This continual questioning of practice reveals constructed knowing as situated not only in practice, but also in time. What is known and how it is known depend on what information is available and the sense made of it at any given time; as time and circumstances change so will what is known. The emphasis here is on "knowing": the process—rather than on "knowledge": the product.

Following the first profile-sharing session with Broadstreet, we asked teachers to provide feedback to us on the process. The optimistic mood of the evening and for the future was captured in one teacher's observation. She wrote: "We all feel confident. We know that we are capable of defining goals and reaching them. We are looking to the future, going day by day instead of worrying that we don't know what we're doing. We do know and are proud of our accomplishments."

Regular Site Visits and Helping with School-Specific Requests. A well recognized prerequisite for collaborative work is the development of trust and a level of comfort that encourages open and honest communication. Accordingly, supportive intervention requires "being there" in the schools on a regular basis. Being there also enables university educators to learn about the unique culture of each school and to develop a shared understanding of ways in which the action plans of each leadership team are direct responses to their school cultures. The frequent presence in schools of the university researchers conveys the value they place on knowing the school culture and their willingness to respond to requests for information or simply lend a sympathetic ear.

The university team's goal was to be in each school at least once each week. While there were a few missed weeks—usually at the beginning or end of university terms and around major conferences—the team logged roughly 60 hours per school each semester and a total of 218 days of visits during the second and third years of the project. Individual university team members assumed responsibility for facilitating the project in each school, with one person taking the lead for regular contacts and data collection and a second person assisting. The intention of this practice was to provide the schools with a consistent university presence and also to provide more than one person's perspective on the culture and events at each school.

The continuing presence of the university team in the schools became a crucial element of the program. Our visibility served as a reminder, a stimulus, and a reinforcement to the school leadership teams. The ready availability also enabled us to respond in timely fashion to requests by the leadership teams and provided an ongoing communication link. Regular presence in the schools equipped us to provide relevant feedback to the leadership teams on their progress toward achieving their action plans. It also sent a message to the schools that we were guests who would help—not detached observers.

Specific requests for help were varied in that each school made different requests, such as facilitating work sessions at school buildings, providing data summaries, and assisting in maintaining teams. They also reflected the interpersonal relationships that had formed among teachers and individual university staff members. In some cases, university team members established close working relationships with the principals in the project and were able to provide opportunities for the principals to reflect on the collaborative processes in their schools and the project-related change (or lack of change) they observed. All of the principals took advantage of opportunities to talk in confidence about project activities. In other cases, university team members established close relationships with beginning teachers that began with interviews and often led to regular, ongoing visits and discussions about teaching.

> After an initial interview with a first-year teacher at Broadstreet, Marlene
> agreed to meet with the teacher to talk about problems she was having
> with her classes. The teacher confessed that she was having difficulty

planning for more than one day at a time and had been unable to locate a curriculum guide. The teacher admitted that she was "living from day to day" and asked Marlene for help. With the support and help of her university colleague, the novice teacher succeeded in mapping out a long-range plan for her classes. But just as important, she discussed with Marlene some possible ways to improve her classroom management procedures. Marlene continued to look in on this teacher throughout the year and was gratified to hear that the teacher felt things had improved. The following year, after Marlene observed a class, she remarked in her fieldnotes that the teacher "has developed an awareness of what is going on everywhere in the classroom. Last year I remember the students in the back row of the room going unnoticed. No one in the lesson today went unnoticed. It was truly enjoyable to see her teach the class."

Providing Data-Based Feedback. As Time for Reflection unfolded, researchers and school participants realized the need for formalizing a process of identifying problematic issues and checking the results of their work. We envisioned the school teams engaged in a cyclical process, similar to the action research cycle, of planning, action, reflection, evaluation, and revised planning. But this project aimed toward doing more than simply solving problems. We consciously attempted to help the schools analyze the underlying, deeper issues that caused the problems in the first place. While we believe that ultimately school problems must be solved by those most affected, we also believe, with Argyris (1970), that an outside perspective is often critical to the problem-solving process. This is especially true with regard to identifying intended outcomes and matching actions with those goals. We noted earlier that one of the assumptions of action science is that both individuals and groups often have limited access to important information that can influence future actions. This limited access may result from ignorance or from barriers imposed by external circumstances.

The school participants had indicated their wish for us to play a more active role than simply to observe and provide resources. The role we devised, following a year of collecting baseline data and gaining familiarity with the schools, had to fulfill both our need for publishable data and the schools' need for additional sources of information. The university team felt we could best serve the collaborative effort by acting as consultants to the projects developed by each school and by providing feedback about actions that were consistent as well as actions that were inconsistent with espoused theories. All participants agreed that feedback was important, although the value placed on the feedback varied among individuals as well as among teams. The university team members agreed to serve as consultants working across the school organizations, documenting group members' espoused theories and observing congruent and incongruent theories in action.

Through our interviews with teachers during the planning year of the project, we documented instances of limited access to information by beginning teachers in the schools and a general feeling that they were not being given adequate information about how the schools operate. Some novice teachers also reported feeling isolated and excluded from social occasions. Action plans for helping new teachers in three schools were a direct result of data shared with the schools at a network meeting in December 1989.

In addition to limited access to information, important information can be withheld or suppressed by those who perceive it as harmful to themselves or others they feel they need to protect. Through careful observation and analysis of an organization's stated goals and the actions they take that are consistent or inconsistent with those goals, researchers can help to identify those areas in which information is needed or suggest ways to remove barriers to receiving existing information. In Time for Reflection, researchers spent their time in the schools carefully documenting teachers' and administrators' ideas about intended and unintended results of the implemented action plans. Gradually, over the next 2 years, a four-step process slowly evolved that met the needs of both the researchers and the school members for accurate information.

First, fieldnotes were analyzed for interactions among project participants and others such as students, parents, and central administrators. A data matrix was developed (Miles & Huberman, 1984) as a method of reducing data to manageable chunks of information about each school, which were shared among the research team for accuracy and thoroughness. Second, researchers studied the schools' action plans and developed a set of *espoused theories* for each school. The assumption guiding this step was that action plans represent stated goals, that is, what the school members desire and value. In the third step, researchers used the data matrix for each school to search for actions that were either consistent or inconsistent with their espoused theories. As explained earlier, participants' actions and the implied meaning of these actions are labeled *theories in action*, and while they may work to reinforce espoused theories, they often work in opposition to them. In the fourth and final step, researchers prepared two profiles for each school (one each following the second and third year of the project) as a formal way of providing evidence from observed theories in action to serve as a catalyst for discussion, reflection, and possible action. The time line presented in Figure 2.1 describes the sequence of network meetings, data collection and analysis, matrix development, and profile-sharing sessions.

The first profile was developed during the summer following Year Two of the project and presented in the fall of Year Three. The second profile was developed during the summer following Year Three of the project and presented after the project ended. The profiles represented our interpretations of each school's theories in action along with evidence of the extent of collaboration, collaborative learning and interaction, and shared decision making. Profiles were shared with the leadership teams, who provided either verification or corrections for each

Figure 2.1. Time for Reflection Project Time Line

Fall 1987	Time for Reflection Proposal is submitted to Danforth Foundation. Leadership teams are formed at seven schools.
Spring 1988	Two network meetings are held to study similar projects. Baseline interviews with 75 teachers are conducted. Three teams drop out of the project, leaving three elementary schools and one middle school.
Summer 1988	Two-day network meeting is held in August with four teams to write preliminary school action plans. Research questions are formulated by university team.
Fall 1988	Network meeting is held in December to feed back data from baseline interviews. Action plans are revised by school leadership teams. Research by the university team focuses on learning to teach and informal collaboration.
Spring 1989	Network meeting is held in May to revise action plans. Senior high school joins the project. Research by university team focuses on learning to teach and informal collaboration within the schools.
Summer 1989	Data matrices are developed by the university team. Drafts of school profiles are developed.
Fall 1989	Profile-sharing sessions are held with four schools. Research by university team focuses on collaborative leadership and learning to teach.
Spring 1990	Network meeting is held in January to review and revise action plans. University team shares what has been learned about professional learning cultures in schools, including collaborative leadership. Research by university team focuses on collaborative leadership and learning to teach. Network meeting is held in May to reflect on project activities and progress. Five schools share progress on action plans.
Summer 1990	Data matrices are elaborated by the university team. Drafts of school profiles are developed.
Fall 1990	November profile-sharing sessions are held with all schools.

part of the profile. Questions at the end of each profile were aimed at encouraging further discussion about the school's progress. In some instances, these questions led to revision of action plans and topics for further reflection. In hindsight, we now view the profile-sharing sessions as key occasions in the life of the project. They illustrate how well professional reflective activities can serve groups of educators who are willing to temporarily put aside their defenses for the good of the group's larger goals.

The profile-sharing session with Broadstreet began 30 minutes late as teachers struggled to arrive at the university campus after a full day of teaching activities. The profile was read silently, section by section. After each reading period, the group discussed the contents of the profile. At times, teachers acknowledged "Yeah, I do that. This is so true—you say you want one thing but you can't do something about it." Another commented, "This is not very complimentary." Following the reading and discussion of the profile, the team used the dyad/triad exercise to brainstorm future actions. At the end of the evening, teachers left the meeting feeling they had accomplished much. "I am very happy with the progress" and "I found the activities very helpful in focusing on what and who we are and what we want to accomplish." However, one person noted that "university people need to become more aggressive and assertive about expressing their opinions. Sometimes you are too reserved."

Change in Roles, Emerging Relationships

As each school developed its own action plan and worked on an individual time line, the nature and degree of collaboration and the time given to professional reflective activity varied considerably from site to site. The matrices we developed were helpful in documenting changes in all participants' definitions of their roles within the project—including their interactions with the university team members. These changes are summarized in Table 2.1. Our analysis of the data matrices and our subsequent discussions with the school participants led us to conclude that project dynamics moved from an initial ambiguity through interactive periods of stress, role overload, and role conflict, toward a shared consensus that the concept of shared leadership among teachers, principals, and university participants was possible, desirable, and difficult.

When we began Time for Reflection, we thought a lot more about how the project would exemplify and foster collaborative reflection than we had about how parity among participants would be achieved. By parity we meant that all participants could expect to receive some benefit and reward for their efforts. We also meant that all work would be shared for an open discussion among the parties involved. For the university team, this meant that our analyses and our writing would be shared with the school participants. For the school teams this meant sharing progress and lack of progress during biannual network meetings. The public sharing of progress reports encouraged revision of action plans and facilitated reflection on actions while, at the same time, making the work of leadership teams available for consideration and possible adoption by other schools. Each network meeting brought new refinements in the knowledge that was being constructed by the group.

From these sharing sessions we quickly became aware of the emotions that team members—including ourselves—were experiencing. All of us had opportunities to practice laying aside our natural defensiveness in order to critique actions and to interpret perceptions. We took advantage of some of these opportunities—but at times we were all too sensitive to do so. At times negative emotional reactions to the collaborative process threatened to bring an end to the participation of individuals and groups. At these times, it was the willingness of participants to talk through problems and confront their pain that allowed the continuation of the project.

We also learned to incorporate celebrations of success. During the biannual network meetings we cheered accomplishments by teams and individuals. We all (university and school participants) attended special events on one another's campuses. We traveled together to conferences and congratulated one another for making presentations about our work. Tensions that often developed among team members as they forged new working relationships were, in some cases, alleviated by opportunities to reassure one another that even though there was disagreement, the person was still valuable to the school, the team, and the project.

Our experiences have convinced us that it is essential to recognize and attend to the emotional issues that arise in collaborative ventures. If such issues are ignored, they will gradually erode the working relationships between and among participants. If they are acknowledged and if resolutions are worked out cooperatively, the participants can become more strongly bonded in their mutual concern for each other and for the project itself.

Looking back, it seems so simple now to relate the development of supportive intervention and to delineate its characteristics. However, it should be remembered that our recounting of this project is a reconstruction of events as we now perceive them, whereas at the time the project was taking place, the negotiation of relationships and ways of working together was a slow, painstaking process. The end result is not always so obvious at the start as it seems in hindsight.

SUMMARY

By adopting an action science approach to our work, we were able to function both as interventionists and as supporters. By formalizing a process of feedback to the schools, we were able to fulfill the need for additional information that could be validated by the school members as either accurate or incomplete. Therefore the process had a beneficial effect on us all—better understanding of the schools' actions for the university members, and in some instances more complete and accurate understanding by the school members. While we can't claim that every project participant joined us in our assertion that problems should be

Table 2.1 Role Relationships for Each School by Semester

Fall 1988	Spring 1989	Fall 1989	Spring 1990
Pine Grove Elementary			
Early role consensus, teachers and principal, concerning priorities set by traditional role definitions. Initial role ambiguity, all parties, concerning definition of issues and responsibility for taking action. Move toward role negotiation, all parties, concerning development of new working relationships. Emerging role conflict, all parties, regarding responsibility for providing feedback.	Emerging role consensus, teachers and principal, concerning role elaboration to include mentoring other teachers. Role overload, principal, concerning the team working independently while keeping her informed. Role conflict, principal and university staff, regarding university responsibilities for supporting project.	Emerging role consensus, all parties, regarding university support role. Role consensus, teachers, sharing of negative information regarding resolution of interpersonal conflicts within the school. Emerging role conflict, all parties, regarding who is responsible for giving public accounts of project to others.	Strong consensus, all parties plus district administration, regarding teacher leadership in mentoring novices. Role overload, principal, concerning duties in addition to school-related responsibilities. Consensus, all parties, regarding teacher assessment of the project. Role negotiation, teachers and university, for sharing negative information with all participants.
Woods Elementary			
Early role consensus, teachers and administrators, concerning priorities set by traditional role definitions. Initial role ambiguity, all parties, regarding the scope and nature of project leadership roles. Role overload, principal, concerning unexpected events at school.	Role ambiguity, all parties, regarding nature and extent of participation. Emerging consensus, all parties, concerning importance of meeting regularly. Emerging consensus, principal and teachers, regarding teachers' abilities to meet and make project-related decisions.	Strong consensus, all parties, regarding teachers running project-related activities. Growing ambiguity, school and univeristy, regarding feedback. Ambiguity, university, regarding nature of support to school.	Emerging consensus, school and university, regarding nature of support and feedback. Strong consensus, all parties, concerning importance of teacher participation in schoolwide decisions.
Firestone Elementary			
Early role consensus, teachers and administrators, concerning role elaboration to include mentoring novice teachers. Initial role ambiguity, teachers and administrators, regarding scope and nature of teacher leadership roles. Role overload, principal, concerning unexpected events at school.	Emerging role consensus, all parties, regarding teachers' abilities and enthusiasm for taking schoolwide leadership roles. Role conflict, all parties, concerning responsibility for sharing negative information with others. Emerging consensus, all parties, concerning university role in providing feedback and working with novice teachers.	Strong consensus, all parties, regarding the importance of teachers taking the initiative on certain schoolwide issues. Consensus, all parties, regarding the importance of the principal as a team member. Role negotiation, all parties, regarding responsibilities for evaluation and feedback. Role overload, teachers, regarding school, district, and family commitments.	Role overload, teachers and principal, concerning school, district, and family commitments. Role consensus, all parties, concerning teachers' and university's responsibility for evaluation and feedback. Role conflict, teachers on and off team, regarding hidden agendas in team formation and participation.

Broadstreet Middle School

Early role consensus, all parties, regarding teacher leadership for schoolwide initiatives.
Early role ambiguity, teachers, concerning individual responsibility for taking action.
Early role consensus, teachers and university, regarding university supporting role.
Role overload, principal, learning about a new school.

Role ambiguity, principal, regarding ongoing participation in team initiatives.
Role overload, principal, regarding new job responsibilities.
Role consensus, all parties, regarding teachers' participation in schoolwide leadership and responsibilities for team designated tasks.
Role negotiation, teachers and university, regarding who is responsible for evaluation.

Role ambiguity, teachers, regarding district-mandated committees.
Increasing role overload, principal, regarding district mandates for school committees and internal issues such as discipline.
Role overload, teachers, regarding school committees and extracurricular responsibilities.
Role conflict, teachers and principal, as team wants more direct contact and involvement with principal.

Role overload, principal, regarding internal issues, such as students threatening a walkout.
Emerging consensus, teachers, rgarding the principal's level of involvement.
Strong role consensus, teachers, regarding the importance of the university's supporting role in working with team.

Fair High School

Early role consensus, all parties, regarding the importance of teacher leadership in schoolwide issues.
Role ambiguity, teachers and administrators, regarding teacher decision making as opposed to counselors' making decisions.
Role negotiation, dean and university, regarding university-led workshops and feedback about team.
Emerging role conflict, teachers and dean, regarding who should set the goals for team initiatives.

Increasing role conflict, teachers and administrators, concerning who makes final decisions about team initiatives.
Role overload, teachers, due to extracurricular activities and end-of-year grades.
Role ambiguity, university, regarding responsibility for feedback.
Emerging consensus, teachers and principal, that initiatives should be continued after external funding ends.

viewed as interesting topics for discussion, some did voice this belief. In her description of insights that came from a profile-sharing session, one teacher wrote that she had learned "that reflection—awareness —is *not* negative." Checking the results of their actions against intended outcomes became an easier task, although never completely comfortable. And surfacing negative information came to be a little less frightening for some. "Being able to disagree agreeably" came to be an acceptable way to move forward during discussions.

CHAPTER 3

Five Schools—
Five Thousand Stories

The school workplace is a physical setting, a formal organization, an employer. It is also a social and psychological setting in which teachers construct a sense of practice, of professional efficacy, and of professional community. This aspect of the workplace—the nature of the professional community that exists there—appears more critical than any other factor to the character of teaching and learning for teachers and their students. (McLaughlin, 1993, p. 99)

In this chapter we want to share some of the pride, the celebrations, the challenges, and the continuing stories of five schools. Embedded within each are the individual stories and vignettes of teachers, administrators, and district personnel whose lives and careers interacted with ours and, in some cases, still do. Because of the complexity of professional and personal dynamics, we cannot use the real school names or real people's names. Our school-based colleagues who helped with this book felt that it would be all right to continue using the school code names we used in all of our fieldnotes—even though those names are known to all participants and a few others who did not directly participate in TFR. Because time has passed and situations have changed, they (and we) do not feel that the information shared in this chapter is potentially harmful to any school, district, or individual.

This brings us back to the "parlor guest" metaphor that we introduced in Chapter 1. At the end of 3 years we had become long-term guests who wished to roll up our sleeves and help, and we wanted to avoid being an inconvenience to the family members. We had gained limited entry into the living areas of each school, which meant continually realizing how little we actually knew about the way things were done and, more important, how little we knew about the assumptions, values, motives, and beliefs that guided the actions of the individual members of these families. Becoming more than parlor guests also necessitated a willingness to lay open to examination our own assumptions, values, motives, and beliefs about collaboration, schools, teaching, and so forth. It truly was much, much more than we had ever bargained for.

While our involvement in the RITE program had provided us with thorough, detailed pictures of the parlor areas of each school, we had only a very limited view of the individual personalities, economic constraints, political considerations, student needs, and moral/ethical issues that influenced decisions and actions. As we spent time in the schools interacting and collecting data, we slowly gained the knowledge and trust that allowed us to eventually assist, to varying degrees, with the action plans undertaken by each of the five schools. We do not claim, however, that we have insider knowledge about any school. We are only family friends, not family members. The writing of this chapter is informed by analyses of our fieldnotes, discussions with participants, and feedback from participants who have read this chapter, but it is still our writing.

We provide demographic and descriptive information for each of the five schools available in public documents and obvious even to a casual visitor (refer to Figure 1.1). We then describe the espoused and enacted theories of teachers and administrators, identified through the data collection efforts of the university team; information about the leadership teams; accounts of the schools' actions plans (see Figure 3.1); and our interpretations of collaborative work in each school. The espoused and enacted theories are especially important because, as they were brought into focus through data collection, analysis, and sharing, they served as the impetus for reflection and, ultimately, action. Readers will note that most of the schools' actions focused on the adults, not on the children. This is not surprising, for the project focused on enhancing learning opportunities for adults who had few opportunities to work together. We will return to a discussion of this phenomenon in Chapter 6 as we consider the implications of this work for our futures in educational research and for others who are engaged in this type of work.

PINE GROVE ELEMENTARY SCHOOL

Located in Suburban School District, Pine Grove Elementary School is surrounded by tall pine trees and middle-class homes with well-manicured lawns. The environment communicates a sense of neatness and order that carries over into the school building. Pine Grove was originally an open-concept school, and the 600 students and teachers temporarily mark off their classrooms with bookcases and other barriers to create the equivalent of traditional classrooms. Isolation often attached to traditional classrooms, however, is resisted by a central work area shared by several teachers within each grade-level pod. Here, the all-white, predominantly female faculty is often found meeting before and after school for a variety of purposes, for the Pine Grove faculty and staff share a long history of collaborating together in grade-level teams for brainstorming, problem solving,

Figure 3.1. Schools' Action Plans

Pine Grove <u>1988-1989</u>

Improved communication and listening skills for administrators, teachers, and students

We Help Ourselves (WHO) Committee uses an agenda and sends minutes to faculty

Guidelines for parent volunteers

Support for teachers new to the school

Involve more faculty in activities; set up a calendar of pod curriculum activities

Walk-about classroom visits

Conduct interviews with novice teachers in building, district, and other schools

<u>1989-1990</u>

WHO committee continues to improve communication

Teachers Learning Cooperatively (TLC) meetings at 7:30 a.m. to facilitate peer coaching

Mini-workshops after school to share information

TIPS booklet produced for new teachers

Increase number of faculty involved in shared decisionmaking

Walk-about classroom visits

Induction workshops for novice teachers from across the district

Inservice for principals in the district

Raise teacher morale through teacher fair, craft activities, birthday celebrations (not implemented)

Woods <u>1988-1989</u>

Improved collegiality through idea sharing and buddy system (not implemented)

School-wide projects to enrich and motivate students (not implemented)

Increase parental and community involvement through newspaper and public relations committee (not implemented)

Survey of faculty conducted to determine needs

Focus on establishing schoolwide discipline policy

<u>1989-1990</u>

Schoolwide discipline plan implemented

School newspaper begun

International festival held

Figure 3.1. (*continued*)

Firestone   1988-1989   1989-1990

Care Bears/Cubs to help new   Training of teacher advisors for
teachers   new teachers in the building

Schoolwide survey and staff   Presentation of induction plan for
inservice day to brainstorm   use districtwide
school priorities without principal
                                     Handbook for new teachers prepared
School/staff luncheon
                                     Conduct interviews with novice
Monthly cultural arts program   and experienced teachers about
to develop self-esteem in students   induction program

Parent workshops to increase
parental involvement in school

Walk-about classroom visits

Cinco de Mayo Festival held

Broadstreet 1988-1989   1989-1990

Improve teacher morale through   Luncheons and breakfasts for faculty
recognition of birthdays; breakfast
for new teachers; luncheons for   New teacher workroom paid for by
teachers   sale of cookbooks, T-shirts

Improve community involvement   Packet of information prepared for
in the school   new teachers

Improve student morale through   Dances for students chaperoned by
recognition of student of the   team members
month
                                     "Night at the Dome" sponsored by
Cultural Arts Festival   team members for students

Improve students' study skills   Open Doors continuedwith increased
through Open Doors study hall.   parental involvement; parents bring
                                     food

                                     VIP tutor program for at-risk students

                                     Christmas party held

                                     "Happygrams" sent for good work

                                     Support teachers' professional
                                     growth through lunch meetings on
                                     selected topics

                                     Increase parental involvement in
                                     PTA

Figure 3.1. (*continued*)

Fair	1988-1989	1989-1990
	Not part of the project during this year	Improve faculty morale through birthday celebrations each month, Teacher Fair,
	Faculty survey conducted to establish needs	Valentine Luncheon, teacher appreciation luncheon
		PASS program for at-risk students: Mentors for at-risk ninth graders; recognition of most improved students by lunch and poster in cafeteria

and curriculum planning. Sharing of professional literature, innovative techniques and programs, and professional expertise is a common practice nurtured by the generous provision of inservice opportunities. This sense of professional community was, however, affected by a large turnover of faculty twice during the project. In both instances groups of teachers chose to work with a well-liked assistant principal as she moved to an assistant principalship and later to a principalship at other schools.

The sense of neatness and order in the building is carried over into the library and learning center. Filled with books, posters, student work, and pictures, all arranged on portable bookcases that sit on a colorful carpet, the room seems to extend an open invitation to come, look, and enjoy. This open invitation continues beyond the library into the bright halls, where each teacher's name is displayed proudly on a plaque with an apple, along with a clever poster containing the names of children in that class. But perhaps the most visible evidence of openness is seen in the area located just off the learning center and used by the music teacher. The area has large glass windows on two of the outside walls, causing the music teacher jokingly to refer to working in "the eye of the hurricane," and it must seem that way to the students inside as visitors peer in to see what is going on in the classroom.

The students are predominantly white and virtually all speak English as a first language. On weekday mornings they walk and bike to school along shaded "greenbelts" or arrive in cars driven by parents. On the school playground they are noisy and active; inside the school they calm down and shift quickly into a routine that enables teachers to function in the open teaching areas. With the exception of the kindergarten, most students can see others in their grade and in other grades as they work. The potential for distraction has been minimized by uniform expectations for behavior—which are posted in almost every classroom.

The curriculum is text-based, but teachers can and do supplement the curriculum with individually designed lessons. On a typical day students can be found completing photocopied worksheets, discussing a story, acting out scenarios to say no to drugs, and conducting library research for science and social studies independent projects.

In this small suburban district, the superintendent has a reputation for allowing each school a high degree of local autonomy. Thriving on this autonomy, the Pine Grove school has received several awards for providing quality programs for its children. The principal's presence is pervasive throughout the building in the high expectations she sets for her staff and the number of staff development opportunities she orchestrates for them. But the faculty and staff are well aware that conditions are not ideal. The principal regularly monitors both positive and negative feedback from faculty and parents, the turnover in faculty has caused some distress, and some students are not achieving up to their potential.

A visitor would not be wrong in surmising that the students and faculty of Pine Grove Elementary have the benefits of an open, brightly colored, well-maintained school with an abundance of materials and supplies. In addition, they have a group of dedicated staff and faculty members willing to collaborate in their efforts to try new ideas and solve old problems. We were not surprised that this faculty and staff opted to participate in Time for Reflection.

Beginning Relationships

In the August 1988 work session activities the Pine Grove leadership team identified building communication and support for novice teachers as primary concerns for the coming year. To improve the former the team decided to involve all staff, faculty, and even parents in a dyad/triad activity in which everyone would have an opportunity to identify strengths and concerns within the school. In addition, a separate committee to facilitate communication between teachers and administrators was implemented. Concerns would be submitted anonymously, and all concerns would be discussed. Another outcome of these initial plans included a request that the university team conduct an "active listening workshop" for the faculty and staff. Once these were implemented the principal decided to wait for analysis of the baseline data before encouraging further action.

In the second network meeting, a December 1988 retreat with all of the leadership teams, the Pine Grove team examined evidence from the baseline data that indicated some individuals did not feel as if they were valued members of the Pine Grove family. Those individuals who were novice teachers expressed concern that their ideas and needs were not always adequately addressed by the more experienced teachers and administrators. Likewise, they felt that sometimes they were not made fully aware of what was expected of them or given adequate time or support to acquire the knowledge and skills possessed by the more seasoned veterans. They indicated that they were fearful that less than perfect performances were not accepted by the Pine Grove family.

There was also evidence that experienced teachers felt communication was inhibited in some instances because teachers were afraid that surfacing negative information might result in reprisals by the administrators responsible for evaluating the teachers according to a state-mandated evaluation system. It is important to note, however, that there was equally strong evidence that these feelings were not representative of all the teachers at Pine Grove. Many of the teachers described Pine Grove as being a very open, positive environment. After a long discussion the team agreed that, since they had begun actions to improve communication, their new plans would center on providing support to novice teachers.

To address this issue, the leadership team agreed to collect data on novice teachers' needs to guide the team's actions. Also, at this time the principal began meeting with the team less, feeling that they were capable of working without her direct involvement. The teachers initiated a survey and interviewed first-year elementary teachers from around the district and from other elementary schools in the TFR project. Having collected these data, they were uncertain how to analyze the results. It was here that for the second time they turned to the university team with a specific request for assistance. Marlene offered to undertake the task, and the analysis was returned to the leadership team. At the time we were unaware of how important this was for our involvement in the Pine Grove family. In retrospect, it provided the teachers on the leadership team with a tangible example that the university team was there to support the actions they chose to pursue. Utilizing these data and analyses, the teachers and the principal approached the district to conduct a pilot project to work with all first-year elementary teachers and their mentors across the entire district. Their proposal was funded by the district and supplemented by TFR money.

As the 1988–89 school year ended, the university team was excited about the progress that had been made since the August network meeting and about the school's obvious ownership of plans and accomplishments. We probably would have continued into the third year of the project with this sense of smugness, if it weren't for the feedback the principal gave to us. Much to our surprise and chagrin, she questioned whether we, as researchers, had actually done anything for the school because we had not met with the leadership team on a regular basis, nor had we been directly involved with teachers or students in classrooms. Instead, we had organized network meetings, collected some data, and responded to task-specific requests. This was not sufficient to be regarded as treasured guests, and the principal reported that she was suspicious of our intentions.

Of course, our initial response mirrored the response we received when feeding back baseline data to the faculty and staff of Pine Grove—defensiveness. Moving beyond this feeling of defensiveness was not necessarily easy. It was only when analyzing data over the summer months that we seriously asked ourselves the question, "What exactly had we done for the Pine Grove family?" and our honest response was, "Up until this point, probably not much!" It was this sobering realization that prompted our commitment of even more time to Pine Grove and the project.

Fortunately, the leadership team was at a point where they could provide us with direction as to what we could do for them. Over the summer some members of the leadership team met to organize and plan the pilot program for new teachers. It was during this time that the leadership team turned to the university team for input, but not direction. The time we spent with various leadership team members in planning for the new teacher program allowed them to tap university resources beyond that of the immediate university team. This was what we had envisioned and were working toward—a professional culture where all members could actively participate in identifying and resolving issues.

Giving and Receiving Feedback

Knowing that the school–university relationship was not as strong as it could be, we approached the first profile-sharing session (based on 1988–89 data) very cautiously. Although Pine Grove was the second school with which we shared a profile, we and they were nervous about the evening. First we shared the espoused theories we had identified.

1. Together we make a team.
2. All teachers and administrators are professionals.
3. Communication is the key to a smooth running school.

Then we shared our analysis of the actions we observed that confirmed and disconfirmed these espoused theories. Throughout the evening at a local restaurant, the leadership team actively participated in the profile-sharing session, questioning our interpretations and providing additions and corrections. Much to our surprise one team member noted, "Last year we could not have done this without you, but now we can." The principal also noted that we were "giving something back to the school." In addition the team began to direct some of our observations for the coming year, noting that we had missed some very important aspects of the Pine Grove community.

While these incidents were seen as evidence of progress, other events from that evening reminded us how difficult it is to bring individuals from different organizations together into a common professional learning culture. Because writing is such an integral part of the culture of the university team, we announced that we should all think about negotiating a book contract to summarize our work. We were thrilled at the prospect and didn't fully consider how the leadership teams would react to our announcement. We were somewhat surprised when the initial response from some individuals was that of caution and skepticism, even when we assured them that all royalties from the book would be returned to the schools.

The initial concern and skepticism surrounding the idea of a book did not, however, seem to have a negative effect on our involvement with the Pine Grove leadership team. The planning with which we had assisted over the summer for the new teacher program continued to be put into action. In the fall of 1989 the leadership team organized and led a districtwide work session on the pilot mentor program. Each elementary school developed its own approach to assisting novice teachers, and the Pine Grove team sponsored separate, monthly work sessions throughout the school year for novices and mentors. During this time we noted that leader(s) had either been appointed or emerged in the other TFR leadership teams. Since this simplified communication, we requested that the Pine Grove leadership team identify one person as a leader or contact person. To our surprise, the team openly resisted this suggestion. In retrospect we believe that their reluctance to designate a leader(s) influenced the leadership that evolved within the group.

The leadership team members continued to use us as resources in planning and conducting the monthly work sessions. The two university team members working with Pine Grove met with the team often, and the team continued to partially direct our interactions. One example of this was a meeting Mary Lou attended. After a long work session to plan a coming meeting with teacher mentors, the team relaxed and looked at Mary Lou. "OK, aren't you going to reflect back what you saw us doing?" Of course, Mary Lou agreed to do so. The team requested assistance in evaluating the work sessions, and we assumed responsibility for analyzing the feedback received from participants. The new teacher program proved so successful (as measured by participant evaluations of each work session) that the district encouraged a Pine Grove team member to assist with including secondary schools in the first-year teacher program. Again, we were asked to assist in the initial planning as the leadership team expanded the program to include secondary schools.

Recognizing the value of the accomplishments of these teachers, the principal encouraged the leadership team to share the new teacher program with other professionals. Through joint funding from the district and TFR, the leadership team shared their program at three statewide meetings. With communal support and guidance, the team members organized their presentations, fought off their own insecurities about addressing other adults, and received accolades for their presentations. These teachers indicated delight and surprise when they found themselves labeled as experts on the design and content of first-year programs.

These feelings of accomplishment and growth were especially evident when the leadership team was brought together in May 1990 for a final network meeting.

- I've made some very deep friendships, learned how to work with people just like me, and learned how to work for a common goal.
- We have learned how to accept and respect each other as well as to compromise. I have been given the opportunity to grow professionally. I have helped others strengthen their skills and my own.

• We've learned to come to consensus. The Danforth team has learned to collaborate to great advantage and we have shared it every chance we've gotten with other groups. We have learned to disagree and love each other.

The Continuing Story

Throughout the final year of the project (1990–91), as the Pine Grove team worked to refine and improve their program for novice teachers, we amended our earlier profile to include three more theories of school success (based on 1989–90 data).

1. Teachers should support one another, but the presence of administrators may inhibit this.
2. University team involvement and feedback can support team progress.
3. Novice teachers and their mentors deserve continuing support.

When we shared our observations of actions that confirmed and disconfirmed these espoused theories, we found it easier to talk with the teachers and administrators than we did the first time through the profile. Likewise, we were pleased when the teachers and principal expressed that they felt ownership of the project. The university connection, which by now had ended, was missed, but not needed. Funding for teacher travel had not been found to supplement TFR funds, but the other plans initiated by the leadership team continued with district support. One of the team members became the Pine Grove assistant principal and several others transferred to a new school. The teachers, even though in different buildings, continued to meet and organize sessions for novices.

At Pine Grove teachers continued to work with the principal to implement teacher-led sharing sessions before and after school. The district further encouraged this by permitting all schools to have locally designed staff development days instead of hiring consultants to run districtwide workshops. The committee to improve teacher–administrator communication also continues. While the leadership team would be the first to recognize that there still is a lot of work to be done, we have every reason to believe that they will continue.

In 1994, as we finish this book, we note that the district mentor program still continues and that it is still led by teachers, two of whom continue to teach at Pine Grove. Of all of the projects in the five schools, this is one example of something that is still operational.

WOODS ELEMENTARY SCHOOL

Woods Elementary School is located in a residential area of Urban School District and experiences many of the problems associated with inner-city schools.

The school could be described as a kind of "oasis" where the faculty and staff strive to offer the students shelter with a safe, clean environment that contrasts markedly with the environment just immediately outside the school grounds. During the project, the efforts of the faculty and staff of Woods, in conjunction with other community representatives, resulted in a community park that promises to expand the safety of the school walls just a little further into the community. With a population of approximately 850 students, the majority African-American, many of the children at Woods Elementary come from low socioeconomic environments where violence and instability are common. This instability is reflected in a high mobility rate and is also evident each fall when typically more than 200 students show up to register after Labor Day, when school has already been in session for almost 2 weeks.

While the ethnicity of the faculty and staff does not mirror exactly that of the student population, it is a racially and ethnically diverse family with an African-American female principal and numerous African-American teachers. The principal, popular with students and teachers alike, sums up her philosophy as: "I wanted to believe I could make a difference. I wanted to believe that there was such a thing as a school where all teachers would be respected and children would be respected." The faculty and staff at Woods have a strong history of socializing together. Many of the teachers accompany the principal on vacation trips to exotic places during spring breaks. They also engage in many professional collaborative activities, as they pointedly told us on many occasions, but these are held on an informal basis. Formal meetings are kept to a minimum—possibly because Woods is a school with self-contained classrooms and because the culture of the school attaches great importance to individual teachers' autonomy. Maintaining this autonomy is sometimes difficult in such a large district where state and local mandates are frequent. In this case the principal has attempts to buffer the outside mandates. She walks a thin line as she attempts to protect her staff and the students while, at the same time, she seeks to avoid being transferred out of the building, which is a common practice regarding principals and assistant principals throughout the district.

Entering into the school building, one first encounters a large, square, open-air courtyard area around which are located the cafeteria, main office, library, and a display case. Branching off this courtyard area are outside open corridors and closed self-contained classrooms. Windows that face the courtyard are decorated with posters urging children to stay away from drugs and stay in school or featuring special events like Black History Month. On nice days, children and teachers can be seen eating lunch outside, taking advantage of the concrete tables and benches. While the openness of the physical plant can be inviting on nice days, it is equally uninviting on hot or wet days and seems to offer an open invitation for the students' outside voices. All of these things necessitate closed classroom doors, limiting teacher interaction and the displaying of students' work. Overall, one does not get the feeling of being in a school until entering into individual classrooms, which are typically colorful and inviting.

Beginning Relationships

While the faculty and staff at Woods Elementary School communicated a warm welcome, the physical plant made it difficult for us to find our way into the living areas of the school. Unlike the two other elementary schools in the project, Woods did not have the open classrooms that made it possible to access a number of classes while minimizing interruptions. Likewise, the fact that the Woods faculty and staff relied mostly on an informal communication system for collaboration, made it difficult for us, as guests, to know when we could enter into the conversations. While we had evidence that teachers came together to plan and carry out instruction, this was typically accomplished informally without scheduled meetings. The culture of the school was such that the teachers' time was supposed to be protected, and meetings of large groups were kept to a minimum.

Our first opportunity to enter into the conversation came at the August 1988 network meeting. Here the principal and two teachers from Woods' leadership team met for 2 days of reflection, discussion, and planning. During these 2 days it became evident that the teachers were accustomed to looking to the principal for ideas and answers to questions. When the tension of indecision became too great, the principal provided direction. While the leadership team was able to discuss problems such as student mobility and discipline, they were slow in coming to agreement as to what action should be taken.

It was at this point that a member of the university team shared with the leadership team an initial analysis of baseline data from interviews and feedback from RITE students placed in the building. As part of this feedback we shared evidence that there was a division of opinion on the issue of discipline and corporal punishment. The division appeared to be along racial lines, with some teachers being more punitive than others. A suggestion was that this issue might be something that the Woods leadership team would want to address in their planning. In the fieldnotes of this exchange, the principal's expression is described as "one of pure pain," while the two teachers responded by looking down and masking their expressions. However, the team did address this issue directly over the next 2 years.

Although later in the meeting the leadership team expressed concern that they weren't making progress comparable to the other leadership teams, they left the meeting with ideas they had gleaned from the other schools and with the intention of beginning a school newspaper and perhaps looking into the issue of discipline. As an outcome of these discussions, the leadership team initiated a survey of the faculty and staff in the fall, which revealed that discipline was an issue that cut across the entire school.

When the leadership team came back together at the December 1988 network meeting, they did so with the information they had acquired from their survey of the faculty. At this meeting the initial analysis of baseline data shared at the August meeting was revisited and expanded, and Pat pushed the teachers to consider whether they wanted to continue in the project. The principals were meeting separately for a time, and this necessitated more active involvement on the part of the teachers. The ensuing discussion among the six female leadership team members present led to a recommitment to participation and the emergence of two strong teacher leaders. The leadership team decided to focus their action plans on developing a schoolwide discipline plan.

During the spring of 1989 the leadership team focused on bringing together a discipline committee to study the issue and make recommendations for a schoolwide discipline plan. It was here that the leadership team, for the first time, turned to the university for assistance. Since Jane had expertise in conducting workshops on classroom management, she offered her services. As in the case at Pine Grove, this concrete, visible example of support from the university team appeared to influence positively our status as guests within the Woods family. As we moved into the third year of the project, the Woods leadership team had identified a specific direction for their actions and were beginning to see progress.

At the start of the 1989 school year, district actions served to both accelerate and impede their progress. In an effort to move toward site-based management, the school district mandated a number of committees for each school, including a discipline committee. The leadership team harbored some ill feelings that their work was taken over by the chairperson of the discipline committee, but took pride that some schoolwide practices based on their work were implemented. With discipline being addressed by another group, the leadership team identified two new projects for action, which the principal approved. They developed the newspaper as a communication vehicle both within the school and with the community, and they decided that an international festival would be an appropriate way to celebrate the school's multicultural character and get teachers working together.

Giving and Receiving Feedback

Things appeared to be continuing positively for the Woods leadership team, and we were looking forward to working with them during the final year of the project. Analysis of the second-year data (1988–89) was completed, and we were ready to share the school profile with the leadership team. Five espoused theories had been identified as representing the school values of teachers and administrators, along with actions that served to confirm and/or disconfirm these values, which included:

1. The principal believes that all children should be treated with dignity.
2. Teachers and students should feel safe and comfortable at school.
3. Positive social interactions among teachers are important.
4. All teachers, including novices, should be given autonomy.
5. Compliance with central administration should not interfere with what the staff feels is best for children.

Pat had offered to share the 1988–89 school profile with the principal prior to the profile-sharing session with the leadership team. After the principal read the profile, she noted several errors and some misperceptions. She expressed reluctance to have it shared with the leadership team because of other things that were going on in the building. Over the next 2 weeks the principal held off on agreeing to a time and place for the profile sharing, even though one of the teacher leaders indicated that the team was anxious to see the school profile.

After almost a 3-week waiting period, the leadership team met with us to share the profile. We met at a restaurant chosen by the leadership team, a popular steak house. Everyone was optimistic about the good food and upcoming discussion. Much to our relief, the leadership team responded favorably to the profile. There were three areas where they questioned our data and interpretations. While we perceived that the teachers did not always have the materials and supplies they needed for the instructional program, the principal and teachers disagreed with us, citing instances where they secured needed monies through creative means such as selling popcorn and pickles after school. We also had a rather lengthy discussion regarding the procedure of taking away rewards that students had earned. While we perceived this as a form of punishment and negative, their interpretation was that it involved learning the consequences of actions. Lastly, they questioned our interpretation that collaboration was limited between and among teachers. The principal and teachers gave numerous examples of informal instances of collaboration that we had missed due to our data collection procedures. The profile sharing provided both the leadership team and us with new understandings that served for future reflection.

In 1988–89 the Woods leadership team accomplished a great deal. With monies made available through the project, two issues of the school newspaper were produced in the spring 1990 semester, with two team members taking major responsibility for the paper. A day-long international festival was held in early June 1990 as the culmination of each grade's month-long study of a selected country. The day of the festival saw teachers and students in the costumes of their respective countries and a schoolwide celebration that included a parade, performances by each grade related to their countries, and professional entertainment. About 3 dozen parents attended the parade and performances, and the teachers held an international banquet in the teachers' lounge with foods from the different countries. The leadership team of Woods had begun to experience the benefits of their efforts.

At the final network meeting, the teachers and principal talked about the effects of the project on the school and themselves personally, as well as their relationship with the university.

- I have enjoyed listening and learning about successful achievements at the other schools and exchanging ideas.

- I was really confused about the purpose of the project because it was difficult to put leadership into our hands. I was expecting the university to be the leader and to . . . give us ideas to help solve problems.
- This program has given me an opportunity to meet with and learn from others in the field of education at both the building and university level.

The leadership team talked frankly about the university team's failure to understand their informal collaborative structures at first, but agreed that once we were aware of how things were done, we were able to assist them with their action plans.

The Continuing Story

Data collected during the third year (1989–90) of the project led to the identification of three additional espoused theories.

1. Informal, professional collaboration among teachers is valued.
2. The staff is concerned with students' success in school and in society.
3. School discipline cannot be segregated from the students' cultural and community norms.

Once again, confirming and disconfirming actions precipitated discussion, reflection, and further action. As the leadership team discussed continuing without the support of the project, they identified the loss of financial support as one obstacle to overcome. Another obstacle perceived for the Woods leadership team was making their efforts more a part of the culture of the school so that loss of leadership team members would not necessarily mean the loss of actions that had been planned. In 1994, as we write this, Woods Elementary has begun to affiliate with the Accelerated School Program, and despite the retirement of their beloved principal, the teachers continue working diligently toward school improvement. The current principal was one of the original members of the leadership team.

FIRESTONE ELEMENTARY SCHOOL

Firestone Elementary, located in Near-Urban School District, sits directly on a busy and dangerous major thoroughfare among industrial-type businesses, vacant apartment complexes, and apartment complexes in need of repairs. Many of the 700 plus Firestone students live in the apartments near the school, so only a few of the students arrive by bus. With no school bus transportation, many parents must drop their children off early in the morning on their way to work, and there is continuing concern about the safety of students in the morning. Teachers often arrive at 7:00 a.m. and open their classrooms so that children can read and do homework.

Although Firestone has many of the characteristics of an inner-city school, the faculty and staff have a districtwide reputation for innovation and excellence. Serving a racially and ethnically mixed student population, the majority of Hispanic/Latino descent, the faculty and staff work to compensate for the problems associated with a high student mobility rate and low socioeconomic status. The opening or closing of an apartment complex can and has changed the student population by hundreds of students in a matter of weeks.

The inside of the school provides a radical contrast to the community around it. A visitor to the school is immediately impressed with the quiet and calm atmosphere that is pervasive, due partly to the wall-to-wall carpet installed throughout the school. Directly behind the front doors lies the central office, where it is not unusual to find the principal as well as the cheerful secretaries greeting children and parents. Two long hallways lead from the front of the school to the open area learning resources center and beyond to the cafeteria and gymnasium. The modified open-concept school houses grade levels within pods that are brightly decorated with student work. Materials and supplies are plentiful and readily available. Classroom areas, separated by bookcases and dividers, allow students and teachers a clear view of other classes and provide flexibility for adding or removing classes. At the end of each pod is a large enclosed room that permits teachers and students to come together for special projects or activities where noise need not be of concern. For example, in the fourth-grade room, a special science project was set up by one teacher for a period of several weeks, and each fourth-grade class was able to take advantage of that teacher's expertise. Each pod also contains a teacher planning room where students are sometimes given one-on-one tutoring.

With the exception of one Hispanic male, all of the teachers are white or Hispanic/Latina females. Many of the teachers transferred to Firestone, when it opened, to be with the principal because of the family-like atmosphere she creates for teachers and students. The superintendent at the time we originally requested schools to participate in the RITE preservice teacher education program told us that he was giving us one of his best schools, and we should not "mess it up." The present superintendent selected the principal of Firestone to be part of another Danforth-funded project involving vertical teams. The projects complemented one another, and the principal continues to be at the forefront of district innovations, including recent selection as a pilot school for site-based management.

Beginning Relationships

As the leadership team from Firestone generated their initial action plans for the project, the manner in which they worked together was impressive. Although the teachers tended to look to the principal for direction, the atmosphere was open, and the goal of developing a collaborative community seemed to be one that they were excited about and committed to accomplishing. Their plans outlined in the August 1988 workshop included activities aimed at helping new teachers, establishing communication with parents, and developing multicultural awareness for the students, faculty, and parents. When they shared their plans, the other leadership teams were openly admiring and talked about modifying some of the Firestone leadership team's ideas for their own schools. In the fall, new teachers were paired with more experienced teachers in what was called the Care Bear/Cub program, and a "Brag Wall" in the teachers' lounge recognized teachers' accomplishments. However, it was surprising to see that the planned actions were not pervasive nor were they moving forward. What became apparent was that the teachers were hesitant to call meetings or take action. They were waiting for the principal, who was busy with the start of school and an influx of more than 100 unexpected new students.

When we shared our perception with the principal, she agreed that the leadership team probably wasn't aware that she wanted them to call meetings and take action without her being present. She quickly realized that her responsibility to the teachers was to give them permission to make decisions and take action without her presence. The principal also recognized that traditionally she perceived her role to be one of "keeping things off them [the teachers]." She now realized that the teachers felt "limited ownership" of decisions and actions in the building. When the principal shared these realizations with the teachers, they began to meet and move forward with the action plans, keeping the busy principal informed of their progress. As the principal described the experience, "I've learned a lot. I see the teachers taking the ball and running with it. As I've let them do it, they've run with it." Over this first hurdle, we were looking forward to having the Firestone leadership team join us for the December 1988 network meeting, which included sharing baseline data.

Joining the faculty of Firestone Elementary could be described as somewhat like marrying into a large family. While the reception was warm, the closeness could, for some new members, be rather intimidating. Although the principal was younger than many of her faculty, she had traditionally assumed a matriarchal role of protecting the teachers and students from outside interruptions. Likewise, most of the teachers were anxious to please the principal and worked to minimize any disruptions in the smoothly running organization. Most of the faculty and staff shared a long history of traditions along with a wealth of common knowledge regarding the way business was conducted at Firestone. One first-year teacher confided to a university team member that at the beginning of the year she thought students were required to stop at every clock while walking down the hall. It was several weeks before the new teacher realized that teachers were merely using the clocks as convenient markers for students. The combination of strong unspoken traditions and the faculty's reputation of excellence prompted some new teachers to feel that they must "prove themselves" to the experienced staff.

During the December 1988 network meeting, the leadership team examined data related to some new teachers' perceptions that they were not a part of the family. The leadership team took this very seriously and focused their plans on addressing this issue. They initiated a survey of the faculty and held a faculty work session. They shared the perceptions of some new teachers and used activities they had engaged in at the December network meeting with their faculty to examine how new teachers could be inadvertently unassisted or intentionally assisted. Although the work session appeared to go well, feedback later indicated that some of the teachers had difficulty accepting the possibility that their actions could lead to some new teachers not feeling welcome. As the principal described it, some of the teachers responded, "Golly, we're not like that." We also began to sense that the university team was being closed out of some meetings. The discomfort appeared to be threatening the future of the project at Firestone.

It was only with the concerted effort of the leadership team, the principal, and ourselves that the project continued. Three university team members attended a faculty meeting where they once again explained the project and answered questions. The leadership team also initiated "walk-abouts," a program for which TFR monies were used to hire a substitute to cover classes so that some teachers could spend time observing in other teachers' classrooms. These events resulted in a renewed commitment to the project, and the leadership team began working after school and during the summer to design a building mentor program for first-year teachers. A few new teachers joined the leadership team, which ensured representation for every grade level.

Giving and Receiving Feedback

As we met to share the school profile, reflecting data collection and analysis of the first year (1988–89), the Firestone leadership team was tired but proud of their accomplishments. Four espoused theories were identified and verified by the leadership team. These school values included:

1. Problems should not be discussed outside the Firestone family.
2. Novice teachers and those new to the building should be integrated into the family.
3. The school should develop positive relations with parents and the community.
4. Innovative teacher leadership is important to school improvement.

During the profile-sharing session one of the teachers again stated that it was difficult not to respond defensively to feedback that could be construed as negative.

The leadership team recognized the importance of surfacing information, both positive and negative, although they acknowledged it was not necessarily pleasant. Rather than closing us out, they asked that we become more a part of their community. As a direct result, over the final months of the project both Renee and Mary Lou were asked to spend time in classrooms observing and providing information and feedback.

Utilizing university team members as resources, the leadership team initiated their new teacher program. Prior to the beginning of the 1989–90 school year, the experienced teachers, called "teacher advisors," held a meeting for the first-year teachers that included "gifts" of classroom supplies and information on policies, procedures, and personnel; a role-play session on parent conferencing; and a booklet compiled by leadership team members containing everything a newcomer would need to know after he or she forgot the information shared before school. The session was videotaped and served as a source of information and entertainment throughout the year! The leadership team also met with the teacher advisors for a work session. Periodic events for the new teachers and teacher advisors were planned throughout the fall, and the program was evaluated by the team toward the end of the first semester.

Members of the Firestone leadership team took on the task of evaluating the induction program through interviews with participants. The evaluation process itself offered some of the leadership team members and us an opportunity to grow. As these teacher leaders designed and conducted the evaluation, they turned to the university team for feedback. Since these were new roles for the teachers, support and feedback appeared to be important. Renee worked with the teacher leaders to develop interview questions and the logistics of conducting the interviews. The teachers' approach was less formal than what researchers probably are accustomed to, and Renee really struggled with her role. At the end of one set of fieldnotes Renee commented, "Now that I have typed these, and have had a chance to think about them, I wonder if perhaps I was too insistent on comparable questions across teachers and written notes. I wonder if I came on much too strong and imposed a researcher value system on a teacher-led, wonderfully informal design? I think I will share my doubts with [teacher leader] and will give her these fieldnotes to comment upon." Renee did share the notes with the teacher leader, adding the comment, "If I came on too strong, please feel free to go back to your own, original idea of just asking people how things were going. You won't offend me—even a little bit." The teacher leaders, however, used the more formal questions, and Renee helped with data analysis. The results of this analysis showed that new teachers felt much more accepted than the previous year's group. They also showed that teacher advisors varied with regard to their availability to reach out to new teachers—particularly when a new teacher was in a different grade level.

Their successful experience with the new teacher program in their building became known to others in the district, and the teachers were surprised and delighted with requests for information about their program. This, combined with an awareness of a recent state mandate requiring a district plan for teacher induction, prompted the leadership team to consider presenting their program to the superintendent for possible districtwide adoption. Thus, some members of the leadership team and Renee met with the superintendent. Although he complimented the team members on their efforts, he indicated that he had other plans. Resisting feeling rejected, the leadership team expressed that they were proud of all their accomplishments and did not feel the outcome lessened their success.

The Continuing Story

As TFR drew to a close, the Firestone leadership team recognized that they had more to do. They decided, however, that changes would necessitate the disbanding of the group. This decision was related to three factors. The first was the end of external funding. The second related to a district mandate for several standing school improvement committees. The leadership team, along with the faculty, made a conscious decision to spread out among the mandated committees and share with the other groups the process skills they had learned through TFR. The third factor involved the lingering suspicion and resentment that some teachers still harbored regarding the motives of those acting as leadership team members. A few teachers still questioned whether some leadership team members were performing solely for the benefit of the principal—who also served as an evaluator in a state-mandated teacher evaluation system which included placement on a career ladder and merit pay for better evaluations. In the final network meeting the team carefully decided how they would work within the larger scheme of school and district committees. Final reflections of the team members focused on how much they had learned about being school leaders and about the process of school improvement.

- People know it's OK that things aren't perfect. Our school is a great place to be. To keep it that way, we must continue to grow and change.
- The team process has been building slowly but firmly. We have gotten to know each other better. We have started to recognize each other's strengths and have encouraged them.

At the final profile-sharing session, the principal and various leadership team members reported that they had indeed joined these other newly mandated committees. They were proud to find that their involvement in TFR had put them "ahead of the game." The Firestone teachers described themselves as "barracudas," lending their considerable leadership and collaborative work skills to the accomplishments of school and district goals. They also confirmed the three additional theories that were identified from data collected during the third year of the project (1989–90). These espoused theories included:

1. Outside funding enables the development of action plans and the implementation of school improvement projects.
2. Teachers who work after school hours on district projects should be compensated.

During the writing of this book, we received updates from the Firestone team. We were pleased to see that they were continuing their work on schoolwide committees and were proud of the leadership role they continued to play in the school's efforts.

BROADSTREET MIDDLE SCHOOL

During TFR Broadstreet was one of the largest middle schools in Texas, with approximately 100 teachers and 2,200 students. The student population, which is primarily Hispanic/Latino and African-American, is very transient, and many students come from low socioeconomic backgrounds. They arrive at school in a mass confusion of cars and buses. Those who walk not only must dodge cars, but must carefully skirt the drainage ditches that line both sides of the road. Once at school they enter a building designed for a maximum of 1,500 students, which is, therefore, strained by overcrowding. Although the structure is well maintained, numerous additions have resulted in a physical layout that reminds one of a never-ending maze. Moving through the building during class changes is difficult as students crowd the halls. Security personnel, armed with walkie-talkies, attempt to monitor the mass of students both in and outside the building.

Despite the numbers, Broadstreet is not a depressing school, nor does one sense despair or anger from the students and teachers. In the office parents are greeted in English or in Spanish, whichever they prefer. Walls and bathrooms are clear of graffiti; classrooms are decorated with posters and with students' work. In an effort to establish closer contact with the students and provide an integrated program, the faculty operates within a cluster system where five cross-subject academic teachers assume responsibility for a group of approximately 150 students. In this cluster system teachers are provided joint planning periods for meeting and planning instruction. This also provides time for all of a student's academic teachers to meet with parents at one time if necessary. However, the cluster system did not, at the time of TFR, include teachers in special-subject areas like art, music, and physical education. While most of the students and their parents speak Spanish as their primary language, most of the teachers do not. Although various people serve as translators, the demand for these individuals is typically greater than the availability.

The large, ethnically and racially diverse group of teachers and administrators has struggled to establish a strong sense of community and traditions despite the constant turnover of teachers and, as TFR began, administrators. The Urban School District superintendent at the time had adopted a policy of transferring small groups of administrators every 6 months. During the time of the Danforth project, 3 different principals worked with the faculty of Broadstreet and with us. Even though principals changed frequently during the 3 years we worked together, the Broadstreet teachers exerted great pressure on the administration to remain in the project.

Beginning Relationships

Moving into the living area of Broadstreet, we quickly found that expecting the "unexpected" was a way of life for the faculty. From new principals to student walkouts, each day seemed to bring a change or crisis with which to deal. The immediacy of many of these problems constantly infringed upon the faculty's desire to step back and do long-range planning. This was the case when the leadership team met in August 1988.

As the team of four men and five women began to lay out their action plans for the upcoming year, they did so with the uncertainty of getting to know a new principal. Because the new principal was not present at this meeting, the teachers had no one but themselves to rely on. This did not, however, seem to impede the progress of the team. They moved quickly, identifying a long list of possible actions that focused on improving student academic performance, student morale, teacher morale, and community involvement. The second day, one team member questioned and challenged some of the ideas that had been generated. While impressed with the insight and determination of the group, we worried about the potential for interpersonal conflict as the members argued and debated possible actions. At the end of the workshop, however, this group appeared to have achieved consensus and a commitment to action. And they ended the day with more detailed action plans than any of the other groups.

Once back in school, the leadership team quickly experienced the difficulties of moving their plans into action while coping with the everyday demands of teaching. As the faculty struggled to adjust to the leadership of a new principal, the Broadstreet team addressed the problems of coordinating their actions and establishing a system of communication. When we met with the team in September, confusion and lack of action appeared to be threatening the group. At this meeting we asked the team members to: (1) list one accomplishment made this year that they were proud of, (2) list one small goal for the group that could be accomplished over the next few weeks, and (3) state one feeling that they would transmit to the group, but might not say face to face. Following this meeting, the leadership team decided to hang together and began dividing responsibilities and taking action.

Because of the number of outside demands, such as coaching, tutoring, or advising clubs, one of the major problems for the Broadstreet team was finding time to meet. Meetings were held before and after school, often with individual members absent or leaving halfway through discussions. In order to move their plans into action, the leadership team divided up the tasks, with individuals assuming responsibility for those areas in which they were most interested. The leadership team usually met over lunch and during breaks in the library. Here an informal communication network was established wherein the librarian, a member of the leadership team, counseled, listened, organized, and generally ran part of the project. One member, a Hispanic male who was designated as a chairperson for the team, served as a buffer between team members when conflict arose, acted as a liaison with the university team, and spotted potential problems within the project before they became serious rifts.

Teacher morale was a strong focus throughout the first year. The team celebrated faculty and staff birthdays, provided lunch to celebrate nothing in particular, and provided goodies for staff workdays. Of all the teams, this was the only group that had no trouble believing that our time and the project resources were theirs to spend as they wished from the beginning of TFR. The team also established an evening tutorial program, a project focusing on improving student academic performance. In the Open Doors program, held once a week, parents could work with their children with the assistance and guidance of teachers. The team also encouraged school dances for the students and initiated special fundraising activities, such as the sale of banners and flowers, which the students enjoyed. These activities appeared to be especially important as the faculty and staff continued to have difficulties adjusting to the new principal.

At a network meeting in December, the Broadstreet leadership team expressed pride in the progress they had made but worried about the atmosphere within their building—the low teacher and student morale appeared to minimize their accomplishments. Then, in January, the principal was transferred, and a new principal joined the Broadstreet faculty. Immediately a sense of optimism returned to the faculty, and the leadership team took advantage of the opportunity. Representatives of the leadership team met with the new principal to make her aware of the group's efforts. The principal's response was supportive and encouraging. The team felt that they had the backing they needed to continue in their efforts, and we were pleased to see the renewed spirit within the building.

Until this time our role as "welcomed guests" was primarily that of acting as a sounding board and as cheerleaders. Most often individual team members sought us out to act as listeners, and we did a lot of listening. In addition, we believed we were providing encouragement and support for the team. After observing in some classrooms and cluster meetings, we were also asked by individual teachers for assistance with planning and conducting instruction. In the majority of instances these requests came from novice teachers faced with the difficulties of adjusting not only to the first year of teaching but also to the problems of an inner-city school. In some instances, however, experienced teachers sought to have us observe and talk about possibilities for improving classroom management and instruction.

While we thought all was proceeding smoothly, one of the teachers shared with us that the Broadstreet leadership team thought we were disappointed in them because they had not accomplished all of their goals. We had underestimated the importance of continually and openly celebrating successes. As we analyzed data from the second year of the project and planned to share the school profile with the Broadstreet team, we saw it as an opportunity to not only provide information for them but also recognize their accomplishments under what we would describe as difficult conditions.

Giving and Receiving Feedback

In the fall of 1989 three members of the team left Broadstreet for other positions, and new members were recruited. At the same time, the leadership team's confidence was once again shaken by outside forces. In an effort to move toward more teacher involvement in the decision-making process, the district mandated the establishment of committees within every building. In view of these developments, the leadership team openly questioned whether they were needed and worried about not wanting to "step on anyone's toes." At the same time, the principal expressed her frustration with the team. The principal relied heavily on the team to provide her with information about the school, but stated several times that they would need to meet without her—she was simply too busy to "chair one more committee." While she believed she had communicated her support of the group, her lack of presence at many of their functions was interpreted by some leadership team members as a lack of support. The profile-sharing session (based on 1988–89 data) provided an opportunity for some of these feelings and concerns to be openly expressed.

In the profile, four primary school values, or espoused theories, of teachers and administrators were identified by the university team and confirmed by the Broadstreet team.

1. Teachers value visible leadership from administrators.
2. Teachers and administrators value parental involvement.
3. Teachers and administrators value the cluster system as a means of improving their teaching.
4. Teachers and administrators value a positive morale for adults and students.

As the leadership team read through the data provided in the profile, there was much discussion. The principal shared with the team her concerns, and individual members of the leadership team surfaced information not previously shared with the principal. At the conclusion of the meeting, the team reaffirmed their commitment to focus on improving student academic performance, student morale, teacher morale, and community involvement.

Continuing with the same informal communication network, the team managed to realize many of their goals. With the additional financial support of a corporate sponsor, they continued with Open Doors, the evening tutorial program. In an effort to build student and teacher morale, the team continued to encourage student dances, provided ribbons for Valentine's Day, sold faculty T-shirts, compiled a faculty cookbook, and organized social events, including a "Night at the Dome" for parents, teachers, and students to attend a baseball game. Recognizing the needs of teachers new to the building, the leadership team prepared a packet for new teachers with general information about the school and school procedures. They also undertook the major task of securing a place in the building where teachers could meet. Since space was at a premium, this was no easy feat.

In November they proudly opened a teacher workroom, which they had decorated and furnished on their own time with limited financial support. Here teachers could come to talk and work with minimal interruptions. Since the leadership team had indicated a desire to encourage conversation and collaboration among teachers, Marlene offered to conduct a brown bag luncheon. A number of teachers asked about taking classes at the university, and Marlene investigated the admissions process and secured the necessary forms, including a class schedule for the summer and fall. This information was shared with a number of teachers during a brown bag lunch during the first week of March. At the conclusion of the 1989–90 school year, the leadership team conducted a survey of the faculty and staff as a means of receiving feedback regarding the activities they had initiated during the year. They were both surprised and excited by the positive feedback and support they received from the faculty. A number of individuals indicated that they would like to be involved in continuing some of the activities the leadership team had initiated.

The Continuing Story

At the final network meeting, the Broadstreet leadership team expressed dismay that the project was ending and requested that the university team find some way to continue the network. They indicated that they valued the planning time provided and confirmed the importance of having time away from the school. This team also felt that their relationship with a university gave them status in the eyes of other faculty members and legitimated action that teachers are not ordinarily allowed to take on their own.

- [The project] has revitalized me—given me a sense of belonging again—given me a reason to care about what happens to [Broadstreet]. I feel like we have made a difference.
- [The project] has given me a sense of ownership toward our school. It's

difficult to sit back and let others do the work in this team. The team has created an atmosphere of caring and camaraderie.

In the final year of TFR we identified four new espoused theories (based on 1989–90 data).

1. New teachers should be welcomed and integrated into the building.
2. Teachers and administrators value involvement of people and groups from outside the school.
3. Increased coordination and communication among groups in the building are important to school improvement.
4. Teachers should play an active part in schoolwide decision making.

When we presented this profile the team shared that they had changed their name to the "D-Team" and that after some struggling they had managed to keep most of the activities going by recruiting new members and by reminding themselves that they were quite capable. They also shared that construction of a new school was underway and that this would alleviate some of the overcrowding.

FAIR HIGH SCHOOL

Situated in a quiet residential corner of large Urban School District, Fair High School offers an unexpected change from the traditional inner-city high school. Surrounded by a well-established, middle-class neighborhood, the school serves a student population of fewer than 1,000 students who are both ethnically and racially diverse. Originally designed as a junior high school, the building includes several open outdoor patios where students meet freely between classes, during lunch, and before and after school. An open campus allows students to come and go, and visitors are amazed by the large number of cars that enter and leave the school parking lot throughout the day. Teachers also utilize this freedom to run errands during their lunch hours, picking up materials for school clubs and projects. The students and faculty of Fair move throughout the day without traditional bells to mark the beginning and end of class periods. Whether because of the small student population or the open environment, students and teachers seem to know one another. Frequently in passing through the halls teachers pause to question, talk, and joke with present and former students. Their actions and interactions communicate a sense of community that adds to the uniqueness of the school. Like other high schools, however, teachers and security personnel armed with walkie-talkies are always on the lookout for potential problems.

Fair, an award winning school, has a long history of pride and autonomy within a district that has not always seemed to value autonomy. The faculty of

Fair, one of the smallest high schools in the district, and the community have successfully fought a battle to keep the school open instead of being split up and re-
assigned to other nearby high schools. To win this fight, the faculty and community agreed to house a branch of a community college on the school campus, a
relationship that has proved beneficial to seniors by offering an opportunity to
begin college work early.

    This is not to say that the faculty and staff of Fair are without problems. The
student population, primarily Hispanic/Latino, has a high mobility rate and a low
socioeconomic status. Some of the students struggle to achieve academic success
and are lured away by the short-term benefits of employment. The result is a drop-
out rate of approximately 25% for ninth-grade students. Functioning within departments, the racially and ethnically diverse faculty and staff also work to improve communication and prevent isolation. While Fair High School is recognized
as a "good school," the faculty and staff strive to make it an even better school.

Beginning Relationships

    Fair High School joined the other leadership teams midway through the
project. After an introductory meeting in April, the leadership team, comprising
five women and three men, joined the other leadership teams in a May network
meeting. The principal had been a part of another Danforth leadership project
several years before and was very comfortable with the nondirective nature of the
project. He assigned administrative responsibility for the project to the dean of
instruction and identified an experienced English teacher and department chair to
act as chairperson for the group. Although the Fair leadership team entered their
first network meeting not quite sure of what the project was all about, they quickly
picked up on the lead of the other teams. They came to the meeting armed with
the results of a schoolwide faculty survey administered to determine needs. Impressed with the other leadership teams' accomplishments and reassured that they
could indeed plan their own actions, the group quickly started to identify possible
areas to address. While all the team members were actively involved in the sometimes heated discussion regarding their action plans, the dean of instruction reminded the group repeatedly of the need to move slowly with well-thought-out
plans.

    At the end of the network meeting, the Fair leadership team had reached ten-
tative consensus that they would focus on recognizing and encouraging academic
success for their students. In addition, they would initiate activities to bring the
faculty and staff together more. Some of these plans were operationalized on the
first day of the 1989–90 school year. As part of the opening activities, some members of the leadership team developed and conducted an activity in which teachers participated in learning more about each other. They made a conscious effort
to identify and welcome new teachers and student teachers to the faculty and staff.

In addition, they planned and held, at one teacher's home, a party for new teach-ers, which was attended by a university team member. Our presence at this party was brought up again and again during the year as solid evidence of our visible interest and commitment to the Fair team.

As the Fair leadership team attempted to implement their action plans, they experienced many of the same problems as the Broadstreet team. Finding a time when all or most of the leadership team could be present was very difficult. Meet-ings often were held in a noisy room next to the students' cafeteria in the form of brown bag lunches that lasted only about 30 minutes. Typically, members were absent or left meetings early because of other responsibilities such as coaching, assigned duties, or tutoring students. Like the Broadstreet team, they opted to have individuals assume responsibility for various planned activities. One group took responsibility for improving faculty morale and communication. Another group developed a peer mentoring program, Push for Academic Student Success (PASS), for ninth-grade students who were identified as at risk and not experiencing suc-cess in school. A third group began a student recognition program for "the most improved student" each month.

Some of their plans were easier than others to put into operation. The social activities for the teachers started early in the school year and continued through-out. The leadership team invited us to all of these activities and always noted our presence or absence. This team leader, more than any other, was consistent in con-tacting university team members by phone to inform us of meetings and social functions. In November the leadership team conducted a Teacher Fair where fac-ulty and staff members set up individual displays representing something about themselves that they wished to share with the students and other faculty and staff members. The leadership team moved quickly in initiating the student recogni-tion program. A girl and boy were identified after the first weeks and during each 6-week period for the remainder of the year. A large poster-size photograph of each of these students was displayed in a central location in the building, and the students were recognized publicly for their improved academic performance. The response from both students and parents was very positive.

With little doubt, the most difficult plan to organize and operationalize involved the student mentoring program, PASS. After looking at similar programs in other schools, the leadership team was still struggling to move forward. The introduction of a district-assigned, at-risk counselor for the building complicated the team's ef-forts as they worked to determine how this individual fit into their plans.

Because of time constraints, the team relied heavily on informal communi-cation. Notices about meetings and activities were communicated during lunch or in the hallways. While most of the teachers were accustomed to this way of operating, the dean of instruction found it especially disconcerting. She started to pull back from the group by seldom attending meetings. On various occasions the dean expressed to university team members that she wanted things put into writing and communicated on a more formal basis. The fact that she was also responsible for evaluating the teachers according to the state-mandated evaluation system contributed to her separation from the group. Because of her concern regarding the "way teachers operate," she requested that we conduct an inservice for the whole faculty on group process skills. Thus, in November Mary Lou and Renee provided an after-school inservice for the faculty and staff.

At about the same time, when it became evident that plans for the student mentoring program were at a standstill, we shared how some of the other leadership teams were using the monies made available through the project to hire substitutes to buy time for uninterrupted planning. The team responded positively to this idea and secured substitutes to free up the leadership team for a full day of planning. Marlene attended and helped facilitate this meeting. During this work session, the team met with other teachers throughout the day and successfully identified 80 potential students, along with student and teacher mentors. They also planned guidelines for the program and designed training for the mentors. Within a week the training sessions were conducted, and the PASS program was piloted during the remainder of the year. Members of the leadership team conducted an evaluation of the program and met after school in May to discuss the written evaluations and the outcomes of the program.

At the final network meeting the other leadership teams marveled at all the Fair team had accomplished in a one-year period. The principal also publicly expressed his pride in the team and promised to locate additional resources for continuing the project. The leadership team, however, continued to have conflict with the dean and indicated that they would continue only if another administrator was assigned to the project. Final reflections indicated the leadership team members' appreciation for the project as a whole.

- This program showed that the university can help schools strive for excellence.
- I was surprised with how involved the university was. I thought you would just write checks. I didn't know you would do as much for us as you have.
- [Participation in the project has meant to me personally] a sense of pride to know that I'm trying to help, a sense of belonging to a specific group, and a sense of improving my own self-worth.

The Continuing Story

Three espoused theories were identified for verification by the leadership team (based on 1989–90 data).

1. Teachers value autonomy within a positive working atmosphere.
2. Teachers and administrators value involvement with the students both inside and outside of the classroom.
3. Teachers and administrators value shared decision making.

When we returned in the fall of 1990 to share the school profile, we found a very different Fair. While the leadership team confirmed the theories we identified, recent changes caused the teachers to focus more on what was presently occurring within the building. Over the summer the principal was transferred, and a former elementary school principal replaced him. This meant that the emerging consensus regarding teachers' and administrators' shared responsibility for decision making, noted in Table 2.1, was no longer in evidence.

The district had mandated that various committees be established, with all teachers participating on at least one committee. Attendance was mandatory and role was taken at these before- and after-school meetings. The campus was changed to a closed campus, and students and teachers no longer could come and go freely. Bells were also re-established to signal the beginning and end of class periods. The leadership team had been informed by the administrative representative to the team that the principal wanted their focus for the upcoming year to be the redecorating of the teachers' lounge. The spirit of the Fair leadership team appeared to be, at least temporarily, broken. Some of the older teachers talked about retirement, while others considered transfers. Although we struggled to maintain some sense of optimism, we too felt the pain the leadership team was experiencing at the conclusion of the project. In 1994, however, we learned that recent district support for site-based decision making and events within Fair itself were enabling former leadership team members to feel optimistic once again.

SUMMARY

This brief walk through the parlors and living areas of five schools does not capture everything that is unique about the schools, but we hope we have provided an understanding and appreciation of their worlds and the challenges they faced. While the five schools each represent very different cultures, their stories bear some similarities. For example, more than one school addressed problems of teacher morale, student morale, community and parental involvement, and at-risk student populations. But the fact that action plans were developed by the leadership teams makes each one responsive to perceived needs in that school. All of the leadership teams identified approaches and programs that were new to the school and were not directly addressed by any of the districts' staff development programming.

We also have attempted to relate the problems and barriers to the collaborative process at each school as honestly as possible without doing harm to individuals. Using a summary format, it is possible to talk of "a teacher" or "a principal" in order to protect individuals. Of course, this format does not allow us to present more complete individual stories. This was a problem for us, because many participants wanted their stories told, but did not want identities revealed. In the next chapter, therefore, we present composite stories—or data-based montages of four role groups with whom we worked. We realize that composite stories are also problematic in that they are neither fact nor fiction, but we were willing to compromise in order to provide a glimpse of the emotions that were experienced by the people with whom we worked. Each composite is followed by a commentary from participants who did work with us and who wanted their identities and voices in the book.

With a combined total of over 75 years as teachers, teacher educators, and researchers, we first began thinking about Time for Reflection in terms of our own experiences as educators. This meant that we brought to the project individual histories in the form of perceptions of how schools operated and visions of how they might operate if reflection was better incorporated into the professional learning culture. Of course, this means that we came equipped with a set of cultural baggage that often we didn't realize we owned—until our school participants reminded us. This chapter is one such reminder. When we first shared our outline and plan for the book with the teachers and administrators who wanted to help with it, they replied, "Aren't you going to write about each school's story?" And we replied, "We were worried about confidentiality and anonymity." They ended the conversation with, "We want you to tell them we are proud of our work."

In each of the schools at least one project-related activity focused on building community among teachers. Pine Grove and Firestone developed programs for working with novice teachers. Broadstreet and Fair created occasions for social interactions during school as well as after school. Pine Grove, Woods, Broadstreet and Fair created structures that enabled experienced teachers to share their expertise with one another. In four of the five schools projects were developed to increase students' and parents' involvement in school activities. Firestone held a Cinco de Mayo celebration. Woods began a school newspaper and held their first international festival. Broadstreet began the Open Doors tutorials and held dances and other activities for students. Fair developed a peer mentoring program for ninth graders.

Creating a positive, nurturing environment within the school community was a value enacted by all teams. This often meant that all of the teams needed to work on creating positive, nurturing environments for themselves, while also engaging in critical reflection. This was not easily accomplished, nor were all participants or teams always successful in balancing progress toward goals with critical examination of both goals and progress. To better illustrate this we move from a rather broad focus on the school to a narrower, more detailed focus on some of the individual dimensions related to our work.

CHAPTER 4

Teacher Leaders and Principals: Leadership as a Process, Not a Role

When the university team decided to write a book about this project, we knew that it had to include stories about the teachers and principals with whom we had worked. However, we also knew that it would not be possible to include all the stories, and we were anxious to protect the identities of the participants who had shared their stories with us. For months we agonized over how best to tell their stories. We consulted experts in case writing and discussed the advantages of writing about single individuals as opposed to composite stories that might combine the experiences of several teachers, such as the case known as *Horace's Compromise* by Theodore Sizer (1984). Finally, we decided that since we could not tell all the stories, the next best thing would be to tell one composite story about each group with whom we worked that contained important elements of many people involved in the project. Thus, we turned our efforts toward writing composite stories of a teacher leader, a principal, and two novices, an academic and a special-subject teacher.

The concept of a composite is not new (Peshkin, 1978; Sizer, 1984) but has not received a great deal of attention in current discussions of the use of stories in research on teaching and teacher education. We developed six guidelines for the construction of each composite in order to preserve a high degree of authenticity while also ensuring confidentiality to the project participants.

1. All data included in the composite were drawn from fieldnotes pertaining to individuals within the role group.
2. The report reflected a narrative orientation and replicated the experiences of the individuals being described.
3. The first draft of each report was distributed to individual volunteers within the relevant role group for modifications and elaborations.
4. The reports were revised to reflect the volunteers' comments.
5. The revised composites were distributed to volunteer participants for their written analysis and response.
6. These responses were edited and published under the authors' names.

In preparation for writing the composites, one university team member took the stories of several participants, categorizing the relevant data using the dimensions of structure, individual differences, interpersonal relationships, leadership, and synergy (described in Chapter 2). Given our earlier analyses, it was not too surprising that the data fit well into those dimensions. A sample story was drafted and distributed to the co-authors, who discussed it and decided to construct all of the composites as arguments for the importance of active professional learning cultures in schools. Using the data matrices that had been prepared earlier from interviews and fieldnotes, researchers looked for examples of each dimension in every category of the outline. (The matrices were arranged in columns with the headings novice teachers, experienced teachers, and principals, so it was possible to look down the column and locate information for each section.) It was not too difficult to combine those teachers' stories into one composite story.

Once the four composites were written and revised, we were ready to ask for responses from the volunteer project participants. In a group writing session, TFR teachers and principals read the composites and responded, both verbally and in writing. After this session, the authors took the feedback from participants, revised, and presented the revisions at a second group writing session. Those committed to writing responses talked about the composites and then wrote drafts of individual responses using a stream of consciousness technique. Following the individual work period, participants met together in small groups, read each others' drafts, and responded in writing. After lunch, another individual period of writing and revising took place, followed by another group feedback session. After the group parted, those who were committed to more writing worked independently to revise and elaborate their responses.

In this chapter we present two composites of school leadership; the composite stories of two novice teachers are presented in Chapter 5. These data-based stories are meant to stimulate discussion and reflection among readers. Each is followed by two commentaries written by participants in TFR. The commentaries are intended to provide the perspectives of some of the real people who participated in the project. In addition, they introduce additional views of the role group represented, which are sometimes different from what we inferred from the project data. At the end of the chapter, the co-authors attempt to link the school stories, composites, and commentaries to the larger educational issues.

TEACHER LEADER: A COMPOSITE STORY

See the whole picture? Of course I have problems seeing the whole picture, but this is not surprising when you consider that I spend 8 hours a day, 5 days a week in a classroom with 28 children. I'm privy to so little information. Sometimes I wish they would realize that perhaps the small picture, the children in my classroom, is as important as what I've jokingly come to call the illusive panorama.

Three years ago when our principal first mentioned the Danforth project, Time for Reflection, I thought, "Gee, that sounds kind of interesting." I've always been concerned about growing stagnant or becoming burned out as a teacher. In my school, the open classrooms, or pods, give me an opportunity to see other teachers, but not really the way I'd like to see them. I mean I'm able to see some great ideas and techniques, but I don't really get to see how they fit into what the other teachers are trying to accomplish overall. We really never have much time to talk except for when we ask, When is this due? How do you fill out that form? How are we going to get this done on time?

And things seem to be getting harder and harder in the classroom. I just don't remember having students with so many family problems in the past. The children just aren't the same. I have more non-English-speaking students and children who come and go constantly. The things that worked before just don't seem to be appropriate anymore. It's true that the state mandates on class size have helped keep my class to a reasonable number, but the needs of the students seem to overshadow this. The sudden increase in the number of students, 200 at the start of one school year, really put all of us into a panic. We had to jockey for space and resources. Most of the time, neither are available, so I'm limited in what I can offer the students. Sometimes I feel like it's just me against the world.

So anyway, the possibility of working with others to find time and ideas for improving instruction or our school, well, it sounded like something worth my time. And it *was* worth my time, but what an unbelievable amount of time. Not to mention the frustration.

The first year of the project was especially strange. The initial planning meetings seemed like such a waste. Part of me was truly pleased to have time away from the classroom. And they even served us meals. But part of me felt guilty leaving my kiddos with a sub. During the day I thought about the detailed plans I'd left and wondered if they were enough. I just knew when I went back the next day, I'd have hell to pay for being out. And I did.

I also felt unsure of what I had to offer. After all, I'd come to think of the university people as the experts. I did consider myself a leader, but what that would mean in the context of this project—I just wasn't sure. The first planning meetings didn't do much to lessen my concern, and really left me skeptical about the whole thing. I'd thought that the university team would have some terrific ideas for us and tell us just what they wanted us to do. They didn't. To add to the strangeness, suddenly we're in a team where everyone supposedly has an equal say and no one will be punished for this say. That really sounds good, but we all know the principal evaluates us. This thought was often in my mind as I expressed my opinion. I wouldn't say that it stopped me from saying what I thought. It just sort of made me more careful to think before I spoke.

At first I think all of us waited for the principal to talk, and she did. That is why I was really surprised when the principal told us that she did not want to lead the group, and that we could meet without her if we chose to. After that she seemed to pull back. I mean, she didn't show up for some meetings, came in and out of others, and occasionally just listened while working on other things. For some reason, I think this helped us believe that we not only could but should function more on our own.

There were times, however, when we needed the principal. It was sort of a schizophrenic relationship. We wanted to function more on our own, yet wanted her support and approval. We also learned quickly that she had information and contacts, especially at the district level, that we didn't have but needed. I guess I've come to realize that as a team member she, like the rest of us, brought individual knowledge and skills that added to the strength of the group. And by excluding the principal, we would stand to lose information that could be valuable to us. So, anyway, things didn't necessarily come together easily or quickly. No, it took time, trials and retrials, occasional hurt feelings, and, yes, even tears.

One thing that did come easily, however, was identifying areas we wanted to work on. Actually, the problem was that we thought of too many. Thinking back, this was really the beginning for me. It was here that I started to see the potential of the project. I also realized that it wasn't going to be like groups I worked with in the past. Unlike other groups I had worked with, this project was asking something more of me—but it took me a long time to realize just what that was.

It seemed to take us forever to agree on which areas to focus on first. I kept silently thinking to myself, "If it takes us this long to agree on what we are going to do, how will we ever agree on the how." But we did. It took a lot of talking, compromising, questioning, and then consensus building. But finally, we decided to focus on helping new teachers and increasing cultural awareness. Of course, what *exactly* we would do wasn't figured out for some time. Even then, our plans were altered frequently.

It was about this time in the project that I realized our team didn't really have one leader. Throughout the network meetings with the other schools in the project, I had picked up on the fact that the other teams had either a designated leader or someone who seemed to have emerged as the leader for the group. I wondered why our team didn't have one leader and, more important, what this might mean for us. But it really seemed to be working without one person in charge. So much so, that when the university person suggested we might want to consider having one person as a contact, we resisted. Now, looking back, I think that not having one leader truly affected our team both negatively and positively.

It definitely made communication more difficult. It wasn't always clear when and where we would be meeting. Because we didn't have the time for written messages, we mostly depended on informal communication. I know this led to my having my feelings hurt on more than one occasion. Sometimes I felt like I was being left out intentionally or that they really just didn't need me. It was only when it happened to others as well that I realized it was our means of communicating that was part of the problem.

Although at first these sorts of experiences seemed negative, actually something very positive came out of them. Over the 3 years, I began to build confidence in myself as a person and leader outside of the classroom. Because no one person led the group, I had an opportunity to jump in with my ideas and share my knowledge and skills when they were most beneficial to the group. I think not having a leader made me less hesitant too. I didn't feel as if I were stepping on anyone's toes when I made suggestions.

When the team began to initiate our plans, the hardest thing was to find time. We already had established committees in our building that met on a regular basis—before and after school. But this was different. We weren't just giving input. We were assuming responsibility for planning, implementing, and evaluating actions to improve our school. We soon realized that an hour before or after school just wasn't enough. The children in my classroom have always been my number one priority. So, to consider taking time away from them was very difficult. I did, however, believe that the team's efforts had the potential for making a real difference for kids and teachers in our school. Thus, I agreed to take time during the school day to meet. My absences from the classroom were planned so that they would disrupt instruction as little as possible for my students. Some of the other teachers in my grade level were very accommodating. They would keep my students with their class for certain lessons in order to give me time to meet. A few of the other team members had student teachers who could cover their classes. On a couple of occasions we had substitutes to free up some of the team members. We also were good at dividing up tasks for one or two people to accomplish.

These meetings weren't necessarily fun. Most often they were hard work, and occasionally, when disagreements arose, they were even stressful. There were times when I asked myself, "Why not just stay in my classroom with the door closed and concentrate on my students?" But then we'd move forward—accomplish something—and I'd feel a sense of pride. My involvement meant the possibility of affecting more than just my class of students, and that really excited me. I also enjoyed working with adults. It was a real eye-opener. Many of the team members had been my friends and colleagues for years, but I really didn't know them. As we planned, talked, debated, and resolved issues, I was amazed to find differences in values, beliefs, and motives that I didn't know were there. I guess I always thought, "We are all teachers, we pretty much believe the same things." Boy was I wrong. It was also neat to see some team members really open up. Each of us had so many talents not being used. Together, it was truly amazing what we could accomplish. That is what I meant earlier when I said that not choosing one leader had a definite effect on what our group accomplished. Because no one person led the group, each individual seemed to evolve when he or she had the talents and skills necessary for a particular task. This way we seemed to build on the strengths of the group.

Unfortunately, some teachers who were not involved on the team questioned our motives and actions. That really hurt. I mean, I was putting in extra time and energy, and it really was frustrating to hear someone accusing me of just trying to brown nose or climb the administrative ladder. I know it bothered other team members too. We really didn't surface the issue with the whole faculty, but we did manage to alleviate some of these feelings by inviting teachers to participate in various planned activities.

It was during these times that we probably used the university team the most. Looking back, the project truly wasn't what I had expected. I was used to university staff members providing inservices and classes. Most often that meant they talked and we listened. I was uncomfortable when they listened and we talked. But they really became the sounding board for me and others. In some ways they also served to legitimize our existence and actions. This helped take some of the heat off us as individuals. We could say, "We aren't doing it for ourselves, we are doing it for the project."

At the beginning of the second year of the project the university team said they were going to feed back information to us in the form of a profile. I was surprised at how direct they were. Some of the feedback hurt and made me feel somewhat defensive. It wasn't that the information was anything new. It is sort of like the dust behind the dresser. I know it's there but never seem to have the time or energy to get to it. But when the profiles were presented, it did open up for discussion some issues that had remained just below the surface. Perhaps it takes someone from outside the school to do this. Whatever, it really was hard for me, and other team members, to see the feedback as information and not necessarily problems. I guess it's just that as a school we work very hard to keep a positive public image. This public image has become even more important to me recently as schools and teachers have come under attack. I came to realize, however, that recognizing and exploring an area didn't always have to mean that there was a problem. From all of this, I believe there came individual and collective growth.

It was during the second year of TFR that I began to feel a gradual change in myself. I wasn't as hesitant to speak my mind. I started to see that what we were doing was worthwhile. In fact, we even started considering that what we were doing for new teachers could be done on a district level. But that meant moving into a whole new arena—one of which I truly didn't have a picture.

We had a high school join the project during the second year. You know, they had an effect on us I didn't realize until much later. As we watched them struggle through what we had already experienced, and shared with them our knowledge, I came to feel better about myself and our team. We had grown. We had learned things. We did have something to share with others from what we had experienced. This sense of pride started to show through in the network meetings as each team showcased their accomplishments and talked about their struggles. Actually, it was kind of funny. There was an underlying element of competitiveness, but in a positive way.

By the second year of the project, the network meetings really felt like they belonged to us. Although I still felt a tinge of guilt leaving my students, I wanted to go to the meetings. I looked forward to the opportunity to have time away from the school to plan with the team. Yes, I valued this time but always felt like it wasn't enough.

The third year of the project was the most rewarding for me personally. We presented our ideas to the district superintendent. Although our plans weren't fully carried out, we had attempted something new. We had moved outside of our classrooms and outside of our school. In fact, we even moved outside of our state and presented our ideas at a professional conference. Don't get me wrong. It wasn't easy. In fact, it was a real struggle. Some of the team members were frightened to death at the prospect of presenting to other adults. But we did it. Once again, we talked, compromised, questioned, and finally worked out a presentation to share with others.

What did this all mean to me as a teacher? It's hard to say. But I know that I changed. I no longer think of myself as being all alone. I know that I have others I can struggle with in seeking answers to my many questions. I'm more willing to try things and take the risk of making mistakes. In fact, I think I gained a little more insight into that "big picture." And who knows, maybe I've brought the small picture, my classroom, to others.

I do think, however, that the project ended too soon. In fact, the project ended just when it was really starting. Would I suggest anything in particular to others undertaking similar projects? Yes, I would challenge them to do what we were not successful in accomplishing because of the short duration of the project. That is, to explore a means of moving similar experiences to their whole faculties. Seeing how much we accomplished with the strengths of our team members, I only wish that we could have somehow brought more of our faculty into the process. I can only imagine the possibilities if we had been successful in accomplishing this.

A Librarian's Commentary

The first commentary was written by Sandra Ford, a middle school librarian. Sandra was formerly a speech and drama teacher at Broadstreet Middle School for 21 years and has been in her current position at Broadstreet for 8 years. As the librarian, she was able to use her flexible schedule to facilitate many of the projects that were carried out by the leadership team at her school.

For me the Danforth project came at a time in my career when I was feeling isolated and alone, like the teacher in this story. As a librarian I had a different set of problems from the faculty and administration. We each had our own pressing needs and not much time for sharing—our successes or our frustrations. My entry into the project came quite by accident. The team was meeting in the library and as a new librarian I didn't want to leave my "space" unattended, so I stayed and listened to what they were doing. The project sounded like the "energizer" I needed and offered me the chance to get involved in making our school a better place on a different level—out of the classroom. I thought I might have a lot to contribute to the project because I am by nature very organized and not a quitter—I would stick to the project until the end.

I, as well as the other members of the team, had great expectations. We saw this as a real opportunity to do something worthwhile like the projects we read about and hear about on TV. Now was our chance to show our talents and creativity. Together there was nothing we couldn't do. I see myself as optimistic and upbeat most of the time, so this project suited me to a "t." I did not have to worry as the teacher in the composite did about leaving my students to a substitute. As a librarian my time was not as structured as a teacher's; I didn't have to be confined to the library; I had the freedom to make my own schedule.

At the outset our team felt a bit of confusion and didn't understand exactly what we were doing or what the project would do for us, just as this teacher expresses. However, as we met with the university support staff, things became clearer, and I was really glad that I had decided to stay for the duration of the project. Many of the original volunteers for the project dropped out at this point. The reasons were never actually verbalized, but the remaining members felt that it was primarily because hours and hours before and after school were required to "launch" the project. Another reason, I believe, was that they didn't have enough foresight to look ahead and form a vision for the school.

Time to plan our strategy for improving the school became a factor almost immediately. We had so many things that needed to be done. Our team decided to have one leader who acted as a liaison with the administration, with each of the members being a leader of individual projects. We all helped each other carry out the projects, but the ultimate responsibility for the implementation was given to one individual team member. Therefore we chose our projects according to our own special talents or interests.

Because of the size of our building and staff, we, too, found that it was not always easy to communicate with other team members or the principal. Sometimes a member with a great idea or some information thought everyone had been told or that the person who was told would pass it along. This is when we decided to use a "round-robin" memo to be initialed and passed on. This worked out well, at first, and then fell by the wayside. We went back to the old method of trying to communicate by word of mouth. This did not always work out and caused some hurt feelings and loss of success with some of our activities.

Frustration came when our team asked others to join us. We naively felt that what we were doing was so wonderful that everyone would want to "get on the band wagon." I remember a faculty meeting where our leader presented the project, and we handed out a folder with material describing all our activities. We explained that we would very much like every member of the faculty to select a project fitting his or her interests or talents. We got response from only two faculty members. After several more attempts, we still could not get more teachers to join our efforts. We even changed the name by which we identified ourselves, thinking that might make a difference.

The teachers who chose not to be part of the team continued to see us as a clique or "elitist" group. I really got angry when they came up with ideas of what *we* should be doing to improve the school, but never wanted to help implement them; they just expected us to do the work for them. I even think that at times we liked it that way. Perhaps we were enjoying saying to ourselves and others, "Look at us. Aren't we wonderful. We're the only ones who really care." Perhaps we, as a team, were sending out the wrong signals. At this point we tried to remember what the university support group said at the first meeting—expect and appreciate small successes. This was especially true when the results were not as grand as we expected them to be.

Before school was out for summer, I sent around a notice asking for volunteers who would be interested in making our main teachers' lounge more attractive and workable. Postcards were mailed out when the work day was set. This project was one that really peaked their interest because approximately 15 teachers showed up in their work clothes to clean up, paint, and select new furniture. The fixing up of the teachers' lounge was a successful effort that was truly collaborative—team members, principal, and other faculty members. It represented a fun time and a sense of accomplishment.

I took pride when things went over well with the faculty. One example was the setting up and decorating of a teachers' workroom on the second floor. Not only is this an example of a success with the faculty, but it represented a recognition of the influence of the Danforth project on the principal—extra space was at a premium and it took a "giving in" on her part for us to use the room.

There were many times that we seemed not to be accomplishing as much as we would like *or* even anything at all. And then we would have a meeting with the other schools in the project and would get "pumped up" by sharing our activities and successes. Although many of our projects were not as large in scope as those at some of the other schools, we were the envy of the other schools when we wore our faculty T-shirts. Worn on football game days and other special occasions to show school spirit, the T-shirts gave the faculty a sense of unity and identity.

As the project continued, the need for reassurance that what we were doing was still what we needed to be doing seemed as great as it was at the beginning. About this time we were assigned to *one* university contact—one that we already especially liked. She made a big difference in our attitude toward the university involvement. She was a constant in the project we could rely on. Her many phone calls and "drop-in" visits kept us from drifting and letting up in our endeavors. There was a sense of renewal each time we met with her and/or the other university team members. Several times we met away from the building and away from the university. These times were special.

As I reflect on the 3 years I was involved with the project, I tend to agree with this teacher—I have changed. I know that I can and do make a difference in the educational process. I know that I have the ability, talent, and time to do the things necessary to affect change in my school. But I also know that I cannot do it alone. It takes everyone working together as a team to accomplish even the smallest success.

As a team we accomplished much, took the time to reflect on our accomplishments, and were able to take a look at our weaknesses as well. As a team we shared in the rewards of our successes and were disappointed together in our failures.

Although the project has ended, our team efforts have not. After a period when only a few of our projects continued, we have "come alive" again and have influence over what happens in our building. This time around, however, a majority of the teachers, administrators, and staff have "bought into" the project. Right before Thanksgiving we had a faculty luncheon that was put together by three new members of the team, one of whom was an original member who dropped out early on. We have weekly team meetings on Friday mornings before school to discuss projects for school improvement. We actually have volunteers to look into the various projects and see that they are carried out. A real feeling of team spirit has been generated.

What is the reason for all this? Why join the team now? It appears to me that the project participants from the university, from my school, and from all the other schools have done their job—collaborative leadership does have a positive impact on the school environment.

A Principal's Commentary

Georgia McGlasson, who has been a middle school principal for 5 years, wrote the second commentary. She was formerly an elementary teacher for 2 years, a magnet coordinator for 3 years, and an elementary principal for 10 years. She is currently principal of a large urban middle school that is committed to shared decision making and collaborative leadership.

As I read the story of the teacher leader, I was depressed by the loneliness and pessimism I perceive in her description of her lot in life. I don't get a sense of the commitment to teaching and to students that I found common to the teacher leaders in the project. Descriptions of the students are limited to their impoverished backgrounds and difficult families, and only briefly mention vague successes.

My impression of the teacher leaders was that they were talented teachers, deeply committed to student success and grappling with ways to share and learn and overcome the isolation of the traditional schoolhouse.

A second important dimension of the project, which I find is given insufficient attention, is the way relationships between teacher leaders and novice teachers helped the teacher leaders. In every evaluative meeting of our group, I heard teacher leaders comment on how the energy and enthusiasm of the novices helped the teacher leaders to renew their own commitment. This interaction between leaders and novices was an integral part of most teachers' willingness to stick with the project during difficult times. The importance of this dimension to the project has become clearer during the past 3 years since our attendance boundaries have changed, causing the loss of over 20 novice teachers. We have truly missed the bursts of energy brought to our staff by excited young teachers eager to try new approaches to working with students.

However, most of the themes ring true. There were certainly many times that we all felt the uncertainty and confusion of exploring new roles in interacting with others in a collaborative process. University representatives, principals, teacher leaders, and novices all experienced the confusion of trying out new ways of interacting with one another, our schools, our districts, and other schools within the project. I was assigned to my position as principal after the project began, so at first I attributed my feelings of uncertainty during that first year to a late start. Later, through interactions with my staff and principals of other schools, I realized that the role confusion was a part of the change process we were all experiencing. While it did not make the uncertainty and confusion any less painful, it did help me to feel less isolated.

Working as a leadership team forced all of us to examine and redefine leadership. Teacher leaders and novice teachers came to accept leadership roles and to realize that the leader, whether principal or teacher, need not be the sole expert on everything. In our school, the nominal team leader was selected more for the ability to work well with all team members than for expertise in directing all projects. Leadership was shared as team members took ownership for individual projects. While I as principal supported the projects, it was clearly the team's responsibility to see them through to implementation. At times there was great frustration that no one person—principal, university staff, or team leader—was clearly "in charge."

The change process, while filled with growth and learning, was full of conflict. The teacher leader describes the schizophrenic relationship between teachers and principals, and the uncertainty about boundaries. These boundary issues emerged throughout the project in many relationships—among all project participants and between those in the project and other teachers at the school. Because participation in the project was strictly voluntary, other teachers questioned the authority of the leadership team to make decisions that would affect the entire school. As principal, I frequently felt called upon to be the buffer between the leadership team and established decision-making groups on the campus. When a district-mandated shared decision-making plan encouraged all staff members to be included in decision making at the campus, our leadership team felt threatened and questioned the role it would take in this process. I think that the teacher leaders were as reluctant as many principals to relinquish control to permit full participation of the entire faculty and staff.

By the close of the project I think that the school people had come to appreciate the university staff as collaborators in school improvement. In the process of collaboration, some of the mystique and reverence for university staff was replaced by an appreciation of feedback provided to the schools and the realization that real change came from within the school teams. We came to see how the feedback we received helped us to refocus on our team's stated goals and to keep us moving forward, even during difficult periods. I am not at all certain that we would have continued with the project had the university staff not been there for us during critical periods, reminding us of what we had said we wanted to do to improve our schools. Recognition of this need for feedback from concerned outsiders has changed the way we collaborate with other groups working with our school and has added an important dimension of reflection to new interactions.

Participation in the project gave us a head start in shared decision making and collaboration, which has been very helpful as we attempt to involve the whole faculty and community in school improvement efforts. Our current school improvement plan includes the same goal areas originally selected as the focus of the Danforth project. Several members of the leadership team who were initially hesitant are now members of the school's shared decision-making committee. They have brought their sense of teamwork to the new group and, because they lived through our initial efforts at collaboration, they help steer us around possible obstacles to effective teaming. While we have not yet reached the goal of full faculty involvement, we are clearly much closer to that goal than ever before. Collaboration and teamwork have truly had a positive impact on all of us.

PRINCIPAL: A COMPOSITE STORY

There was a time when I believed that a principal runs a school. Since then I've learned that my notion of "running" a school was a rather simplistic view of the kind of leadership a principal needs to provide in a school today. I've also learned that principals who are foolish enough to try "running" a school end up being runners themselves, moving ever faster, working ever harder to keep up with the demands of their job.

If the Time for Reflection project has had any payoff for me in terms of my growing as a professional—and I might add as a person too—it is in providing me with opportunities to examine my own leadership as a principal and to consider different views about the kinds of leadership that it takes to make a school a better place to learn and work, not just for students but also for teachers and administrators.

Traditional Preparation. I think it's fair to say that my background prepared me to be a traditional top-down principal. I got consistent information about how to lead a school from several sources, probably most important from the examples of the principals I worked for when I was a teacher, but also from the university courses I took to qualify for state certification as a principal and from the various meetings and training sessions that my school district requires principals to attend. I was taught that a principal should be perceived as the ultimate authority in a school, as the final decision maker, and as the single source for coordination of all of the instructional and organizational matters in the school. I say *perceived*, because it quickly becomes clear to anyone who has ever thought seriously about a principal's job that much of what goes on in a school either is prescribed by legislation, policy, or curriculum, or occurs behind closed classroom doors. In either case a principal's authority and control are limited. So to remain in charge, a principal has to be very good at creating internal structures and policies that maintain an illusion of real power.

Maybe there was some past golden time when principals could take complete charge of running schools, but I think it was only in places where both the schools and the communities they served were small, tightly knit, and homogeneous. Schools today are large, and they are part of larger organizations: school districts. A principal really doesn't have all that much discretionary authority left. Plus, a principal is no longer able to confidently predict or manage the actions and reactions of students and faculty who are increasingly diverse in terms of their backgrounds, their values, and their behavior. The old choices of top-down leadership styles, harsh bureaucratic control, or charming human relations persuasion only seem to intensify the differences and divisions that already exist among people in a school. Principals need to know about and practice new forms of leadership that are more about cooperation than about control. The Time for Reflection project encouraged me and my faculty to consider what such new forms of leadership might look like.

Shared Responsibility. At some unspoken level I'd always been concerned about what it means to be a principal and how to be a better one. Events in recent years, however, have made me more consciously aware of how doing things the way I'd always done them was not always in the best interests of the school or anyone in it, including me, and in fact might no longer be possible. For one thing, increased legislation governing curriculum, testing, and school management means that as a principal I have greater accountability for record keeping than ever before. Much of the mail that arrives each day is paperwork that either the district, the state, or the federal government requires. Since I am the one who will be held accountable, I've always thought it was my job to do most of that paperwork. It's very time-consuming and means that I have to be an expert on the status of every program in the school. In addition, it seems that I am called away from the school more frequently for meetings at the central office. I worry that while I'm away things I need to deal with won't get done, and teachers will think I'm not attending to my job.

The Time for Reflection project has led me to question whether I really need to be an expert on everything and be the one who has to handle every situation, or whether I just have to be *informed*. There is a big difference, and it's based in trust. I have to trust that my faculty is capable of doing what is required of them and that they take responsibility for doing things in ways that are consistent with policies. When I think about it, though, my faculty as a whole deserves my trust. They want to do a good job. I know, for instance, that those teachers who are really good in their fields will serve as examples and guides for others who aren't as skilled or are still learning. I am also confident that my teachers won't let anything get so far out of line that it will jeopardize the kids or the school.

So what does such trust mean at a practical level? It's not that I no longer have to take responsibility or that I'm not ultimately accountable for what goes on in the school. It just means that I don't have to know and do everything myself. I can rely on teachers' knowledge and expertise in addition to my own. I can ask them for information I need to complete paperwork, without feeling that I'm revealing some inadequacy. I can seek their advice on how to organize programs or deal with problems, and recognize that I am sharing responsibility, not abdicating it. The Time for Reflection project not only helped bring about these changes in my thinking, but also provided me with good examples of the results of these changes. I have seen teachers on the leadership team take charge of developing programs for mentoring new teachers and for identifying new approaches to getting parents involved in the school and their children's learning, which I would never have been able to do on my own. These successes reassure me. They support me and motivate me as I work to become a principal who recognizes that many people need to take part in the leadership of this school.

Shared Leadership. During the past decade continual pressure has been placed on principals to be the instructional leaders of their schools. In theory I totally agree with this idea; I wholeheartedly believe that the best way for principals to spend their time is helping teachers do their jobs better. In fact, this was the part of being a principal that I always thought I could do better than the principals I worked for. In reality, however, there is simply not enough time in the day to do all that I'd like to do and all that needs to be done for my teachers. Even an elementary principal with fewer than 30 teachers can't always make time in a day to do anything more than spend a few minutes informally visiting a few classrooms, and talk casually with faculty about their teaching in the office, halls, or lounge. This is hardly what I envision when I think of instructional leadership.

What I would like to do is work intensively with teachers, plan good lessons with them, observe them, and talk about specifics of their teaching, reinforcing the things done well and figuring out ways to do some things better. Ideally, I want to do this with every teacher, but I think it's essential for the new teachers in my building, and I'm not able to make time to do these things on a regular basis even with them. Well, maybe if they're in real trouble, I will work with them; but if they don't catch on pretty quickly to what it takes to teach and to manage a classroom, I simply don't have the time to teach them what they should have learned in college. After I've visited a new teacher's classroom and seen her having trouble—usually with classroom management—I'll tell her what she needs to do to get the children to behave and pay attention. I'll try to go back to observe the class a few times, and I'll tell her mentor and other good teachers to look out for her and give her their advice. After that, if she doesn't improve, I have to admit I'll probably become rather cool toward her and even subtly (or directly if she's really bad) encourage her to transfer to another school. I know this sounds rather cruel, but the reality of schools is that neither I nor anyone else can do his own job and help someone else do hers.

Experienced teachers get even less of what I think of as real instructional leadership from me. Sure, I can rationalize that they don't need it; some of them are better teachers than I was—and I was good! But I can remember as a teacher thinking it would be nice to have someone around to keep me sharp: to give me new ideas or lesson materials, or ask a question about something I did in my class that would get me thinking in new ways. I never got that from a principal, just from a few fellow teachers, but they didn't see me teach; they had their own classrooms that I never saw either.

I do see the experienced teachers and I talk with them, and of course I evaluate them, so I have a pretty good sense of what they are doing. But again, it's only if someone's in trouble, like a teacher new to the building or someone parents have complained about, that I'll spend much time in his classroom, and then it's often to put pressure on so he'll leave, or to gather the documentation I need to either support him or read him the riot act.

Most of the time I spend with experienced teachers is in committee meetings, project meetings, or team leader meetings. Actually, these meetings account for several hours of every week, so I do have a real sense of what's going on and can make sure that things are moving along as I think they should. I have always believed that I need to be at all of these meetings and that I am the one to create agendas and set courses of action. I need to be at meetings to give direction and get information. I consider directing meetings an important way for me to exercise my instructional leadership.

There are also some other things I do that I think show that I care about the teaching that goes on in the school. I make it a point to leave complimentary notes in teachers' mailboxes when I've made informal visits to classes or just been walking through the building and seen them doing some really good teaching. I'm also invited to classrooms for special events or to celebrate special student accomplishments. I love these times and the special bond that I feel with the teachers and students. You can't imagine, for example, how exciting it is to have a teacher call me to her class to hear a student who a few months ago could barely speak or read English, read a passage aloud to the class and then describe the ideas in his or her own English words. Another thing I have done is be a teacher myself. Once in a while I cover a teacher's class so the teacher can be somewhere else, but what I think really shows my commitment to teaching is that once every few weeks I go to a different classroom to teach a special art appreciation lesson as part of a districtwide arts in the school program that our school takes part in.

Even though I can point to all these things I do in the name of instructional leadership, when I look critically at how much actual time I'm spending on these activities I know it's not enough to make a real difference or to make me a real instructional leader. During the Time for Reflection project I've been rethinking my assumption that a principal is the single source of instructional leadership in a school. I realize that even though in making sure that I am the only one who sets direction and provides information, I've had the best intentions of my teachers at heart, I have made it difficult for them to release talents they have and to make some of the contributions that they can to the school.

I'd always believed that as principal I needed to be a buffer for the teachers, to make sure that they weren't being asked to do things beyond teaching their classes. Anything other than directly teaching students was my responsibility or some other professional or staff person's. I thought I was protecting my teachers and helping them do their jobs, but now I think I may have been fostering in them an unhealthy kind of dependence that would ensure that my directions and my authority remained unquestioned. What really drove home to me how dependent I expected teachers to be on my leadership was a conversation with Renee, one of the university team members, in which I admitted that I hadn't called a leadership team meeting in a while. When she asked me if the teachers themselves would ever call a meeting, it was like a light went on in my head, and I realized that I hadn't really accepted the main point of the Time for Reflection project, which was that the team was to make decisions. I was still holding on to my position of absolute authority to dictate and direct the actions of the team.

After that insight, I tried gradually to ease up on the reins of control. I encouraged the team to call meetings and meet without me. I also encouraged them to keep me informed about their meetings and their plans, which they did. As I watched these teachers, who had always looked to me to make the decisions, accept leadership responsibility themselves, as I listened to their ideas during the leadership team meetings I did attend, and as I observed their ideas take programmatic shape, I humbly came to realize that a principal who is a real instructional leader recognizes the many ways in which teachers can make valuable contributions to their school. I came to see how things that I had thought only I could deal with because they weren't part of a teacher's job, like helping new teachers, were perceived by teachers as important for them to do themselves. They appreciated such opportunities to share their knowledge and welcomed the authority to make decisions and take action in order to quickly and effectively get their plans and ideas working in the school.

I can see that in some ways having more authority and responsibility can actually make teachers' jobs easier. When they have the freedom to adapt their teaching environment to their own needs, teachers are able to make changes and decisions more quickly than is possible in a top-down system. They are also encouraged to provide the kind of resources for each other that previously I had thought only I could provide.

As I've come to recognize the benefits of teachers' involvement in instructional leadership, I have also become aware of a dilemma that I'm now struggling with. On the one hand I appreciate the quality of the contributions teachers can make as they assume shared responsibility for instructional leadership. On the other hand I still worry about teachers being overburdened. How much time can a teacher give to school matters that aren't directly related to classroom teaching? How many meetings before or after school can he attend, how many special task forces can he serve on, how many projects can he be involved in before either his teaching suffers or he is exhausted or both? I don't have answers yet to these questions, and neither do my teachers. All we can do at this point is remain sensitive to our own limits and to the demands on our time and continually try to maintain a healthy balance. What I am beginning to do, though, and what I'm also seeing teachers do as we seek that healthy balance is ask new questions about how best to spend our time and where best to focus our energies. I am coming to consider these questions central to the new kind of collaborative leadership we are developing.

Accountability. One of the most difficult challenges I face as a principal is that today the performance of schools is being measured more extensively than ever before. District, statewide and national testing of students has become a major concern and often a source of considerable distress for principals and teachers. Scores from these tests are used by district officials to judge the relative success of schools and often can be the basis for decisions that jeopardize or promote a principal's career and to some extent a teacher's. Even more threatening to teachers and administrators alike is the habit local newspapers have of printing these test scores in ranked order, thus leading the public to draw conclusions about the quality of schools based on unfair comparisons of students.

As a principal I face a difficult challenge trying on the one hand to do everything I can so students in my school do as well as possible on tests. I provide teachers with any information I can about the tests and make sure that they are familiar with the material the tests will cover so they know what they need to teach. I also direct teachers to inservices that will help them better prepare students for these tests, and sometimes bring presenters to the school to help teachers teach for higher test scores. On the other hand, even as I do these things I wonder if I'm being unfair to the teachers and the students. I wonder if I am denying teachers the right to make professional judgments about what and how best to teach their students. I worry that by focusing so much attention on standardized measures of achievement, I am supporting a testing system that by its very design punishes students who suffer from handicaps of poverty, bad home and neighborhood environments, or a lack of English language skills. And finally, I fear I am penalizing the teachers of these students and delivering a message I don't mean to send: that teaching those youngsters who are most in need and at risk isn't worthwhile because it isn't rewarded.

I wish I could say that thanks to the Time for Reflection project I have been able to resolve my conflicted thoughts about the greater accountability that standardized testing places on us and about the way that these tests are driving the curriculum that we teach. I haven't; I remain torn between wanting to make sure the numbers from our school look good, and worrying about what the emphasis on testing is doing to morale. What has happened, however, is that I have come to realize that I don't have to deal with these conflicts alone. They concern the entire school and as such need to be out in the open for all of us to talk about. As part of my changing views on school leadership, I am beginning to see that a principal does a disservice by fostering a policy of silence about problematic issues such as the role of standardized testing. Even though greater openness about this particular problem hasn't led to any clear-cut solutions, it has, I think, helped both the faculty and me better understand the nature of the problem and the sources of our uneasiness. It has also encouraged us as we work together to think of new and better ways to meet the needs of our students and to make sure we give them the best education we can.

Another area of greater accountability that both principals and teachers have faced in recent years is mandated teacher evaluation programs. As a principal I am required to evaluate teachers using an instrument prescribed by the state. The rating a teacher receives is then used to determine career ladder placement and corresponding pay increments. I resent having to use the same instrument to evaluate a teacher in any kind of teaching situation. Even though I try as hard as I can to be fair and I think my teachers know that, when I walk into a classroom for a scheduled evaluation a look of anxiety crosses the faces of even the best teachers. Sometimes I wonder if it is only anxiety I see or if there isn't also a mirroring of some of my own resentment of a process that maintains an uncomfortable hierarchy between teachers and their principal.

The mandated evaluation system is supposed to achieve higher levels of accountability from teachers and from principals for teachers' performance in their classes. What I see it doing, though, is maintaining the kind of administrative control and teacher subservience that I have been trying to break down during the Time for Reflection project. I think that teachers are more apt to be accountable for what they do when they feel it is safe to talk with administrators and other teachers about the questions and problems that arise in the course of their teaching and when they are able to take the risks involved in trying and learning new instructional strategies. Such openness isn't going to happen when the bottom line is that the principal makes a final judgment of a teacher's performance based on what goes on in a single lesson. What teacher in her right mind is going to risk prejudicing what the principal sees in that lesson by exposing doubts and possible shortcomings about her teaching?

I think it is worth pointing out that at no time during the Time for Reflection project did the leadership team choose to address issues of the instruction that occurs in the school. Yes, there was attention paid to mentoring new teachers and to events like an international festival that had learning payoff for the students, but these projects weren't focused specifically on teaching, but rather were directed at enhancing the culture of the school for teachers and students. I can only guess, but I think that one of the reasons instruction was never a topic for the leadership team is that the evaluation system encourages teachers to protect the privacy of what they do behind their classroom doors.

When I think about my responsibilities, as principal, for greater accountability for student achievement and teacher performance, I am certainly not opposed to either. It's just that current measures aren't giving me or my teachers the information we really need. If teachers are to improve and students are to make progress, then the data from teacher evaluations and student performance measures need to come from a wide range of sources, and administrators and teachers need to have some control over identifying what sources will be most appropriate for them and their students. In addition, there must be an end to wielding the results of evaluations of teachers and students as a club over the heads of principals and teachers. Rather, the information should be thought of as providing us with questions, not answers, about our performance, and we should be able to use it to help us develop better programs to help students learn and teachers grow.

Site-Based Management. There was a fortunate coincidence between the Time for Reflection project and school districts' growing interest in site-based management. The opportunities that the project provided me and other members of the leadership team to learn about and practice collaborative decision making and shared leadership have, I think, given our school a decided advantage as we prepare to implement district requirements for site-based management.

I know, for example, that my own thinking about teachers' capabilities has changed. I'll confess that at the beginning of the Time for Reflection project I was not all that convinced that teachers could really handle the kinds of decision making that are necessary to administer a school. My skepticism was based on what I had seen as teachers' reluctance and sometimes even their inability to make decisions at all. Time and time again, I had seen teachers wait for me to tell them what to do, and when I had tried to give them opportunities to make their own decisions, I had seen them become deadlocked trying to reach a decision on what I thought were simple and even trivial matters. I had also seen them make what I considered bad decisions, such as their resolution of our shortage of classroom space: The teachers decided that new teachers should not have assigned rooms but be required to "float" from classroom to classroom throughout the day.

What I came to understand during the Time for Reflection project is that teachers have in many ways operated within a world of their own and it is one that often differs from an administrator's world. For one thing teachers tend to have a narrower field of vision. They traditionally think in terms of *their* classroom and *their* students, and weigh decisions in these terms. Administrators, on the other hand, have to focus on the school as a whole and make decisions accordingly. These differing perspectives can be a source of frustration and even conflict for both teachers and administrators. Teachers may try to protect their turf by not being open with administrators about what goes on in their classrooms. They may come to see an administrator only as someone to discipline problem students, not as an instructional resource. Administrators, for their part, may look down on teachers and think them incapable of seeing the whole picture. Such an attitude can provide administrators with a rationale for maintaining the status quo and allow them to justify their control of decision making and other aspects of leadership in the school.

Working with a school leadership team that was created as part of the Time for Reflection project gave both the teachers and me an opportunity to see that there are benefits to considering each other's perspectives as we work together to develop and enact plans for our school. Insofar as such collaboration is also essential to site-based management and is even expanded to include parents, students, and community representation, we have a positive experience to build on. We have come to recognize that taking varying perspectives into account can lead to better decision making. Not only are such decisions more likely to be acceptable, they are also more likely to be implemented because they reflect and serve the interests of the people responsible for putting them into action.

Something else we have learned that better prepares us for site-based management is that collaboration is a key ingredient of good long-range planning. When I think back on all the years that I took almost exclusive responsibility for developing the campus plan for our school, I have to admit that it was primarily a paper exercise. The teachers weren't very familiar with those plans and didn't think they were very important because as teachers they had at best a token role in developing them. Now that I have seen what can be accomplished when teachers are genuinely involved in making plans and decisions, I can see us developing a long-range campus plan that reflects our genuine commitment and helps us work toward our school goals with more focus and direction.

A Principal's Commentary

Gayle Holder is the principal at Firestone Elementary School. Prior to becoming a principal 14 years ago, Gayle was an elementary classroom teacher. She continues to be involved in several districtwide school improvement projects.

This story is reflective of me. I have felt and made these changes through my years as Principal.

In the beginning, I felt that as the person in charge my role was to keep everybody happy, see all, do all, make everything perfect for the teachers—keep the school "ship shape." If I had all the answers and could take care of the "extras," they could teach. If I could be a strong disciplinarian for them, they could teach. If I could always be happy, positive, and in control of things, they could teach. I still believe this—the feeling, tone, and building climate should be set by me. If I could make our school a utopia for them, then I would consider myself successful. Before this project I felt it was my responsibility to singlehandedly create this atmosphere. The Time for Reflection project made me see myself through their eyes. I came to discover that I did *not* have to create a utopia, nor was it necessary to do everything myself.

I had always told the staff, "There's no such thing as a problem—only an area of concern." The only way to fix it is to know it. As surveys and building interviews were done, concerns (problems) surfaced. Several teachers felt defensive about the concerns that were brought to the surface. They either didn't agree, didn't see it that way, thought it was someone else's fault, and/or defended the reason these concerns were there! A key point at this stage was not to lay blame or say it wasn't so—if it was someone's perception it was also a reality. So it was time to fix it and work on a solution. The fix-it mode forced some teachers to open up and take new looks at themselves as teachers. They began to see the role they needed to change toward, for their own growth as well as the improvement of the school. It was very important at this point in the process that I encourage and support so that these changes could occur.

Now, a committee of teachers has been established to collect feedback and data, and then bring back a *decision,* not thoughts for me to base a decision on. I can say honestly that teachers want to be in the decision-making loop. I have learned to let go, to be a risk taker and to ask myself, "Why not—why can't it be done? Let's try it."

Teachers must be accountable for students' progress—they can no longer blame the system because we now have the power to adapt our system to meet our needs and the needs of our students. Yes, there are constraints, and we have had to learn how to work within those constraints. Frustration was definitely felt with the external emphasis on test scores. Students were penalized, not because they didn't know the information, but because they didn't understand the way a question was asked or a test was formated. Students who might not have been able to read on the third-grade level at test time were still required to take the third-grade, state-mandated test.

The role of the principal in the site-based management process is to facilitate change—but not be the authority or sole policy maker. To be able to facilitate change a person must also be reflective, open to change, and a risk taker. Too often principals have the feeling that site-based decision making means decisions are made at the site by the person in charge, the principal. NOT! In order to effectively change (not only the educational process, but also personal perspectives of that same process), we must not only involve but collaborate with a *cadre* of those involved—teachers, staff, parents, and community. *Involving* an array of individuals in the site-based, decision-making process increases buy-in and ownership of the system and ultimately its success. The strength of a system lies in the satisfaction (success) of its customers.

Even with site-based management, we still must stay within the guidelines imposed by state and local mandates. We must be accountable and professional to ensure that changes we want to make will be effective, and be able to document that effectiveness.

The staff of Firestone has definitely benefited from the project in a multitude of ways. The Time for Reflection experience was definitely a presite-based management exercise for Firestone Elementary. But now, because of the project, I'm further into the process of site-based management. I still struggle with "letting go" but enjoy it when I do.

A Teacher's Commentary

The second commentary was written by Jacquelyn Hinojosa, a third-grade teacher with 25 years experience. During the project she was a member of Pine Grove's leadership team and worked in her district to help establish a mentoring program for elementary and secondary novice teachers. She is still active in that program.

This story brings back memories of the principal's role in the Time for Reflection project. All of the principals I have worked for or with in my 25 years of teaching seem to have been the same broad personality type—extrovert, leader, quick to make decisions, exuding ideas (but not particularly wanting to work out the details of the ideas), not particularly liking to be questioned about their decisions. When I try to look at their job objectively, I can see what an awkward position they are often in, with parents, students, teachers, community, and the district administration depending on them as the leader and decision maker of the school.

A few principals I have talked to privately have shared instances with me of members on the staff who are at different levels professionally. Some are at the first level, still thinking only of themselves (no matter how long they have been teaching), and others are able to rise above themselves and think of the bigger picture and the benefit to the entire school. I think this is one reason that it is difficult for the principal to hand over some of his or her authority.

I hope the project has helped the principals in TFR become aware that they do not need to be an expert in every area. My principal has shared that in her interviewing and hiring she tries to hire the best possible people for our school community and then she trusts them to do their job. This sometimes is a problem when a teacher who is left alone to do his job feels neglected and would like more communication and positive feedback from the principal. I think it is important for the principal to meet with individual teams once each 6-week period so that the principal can be informed of what's going on in the school. It is also important for the principal to meet more often with the whole staff to give them incoming information that they need to do their jobs effectively.

The more everyone in the school is involved in making decisions about which programs to develop and to implement in their school, the more everyone buys into a program and is excited and enthusiastic about carrying out the program. This enthusiasm will carry over to the students and to the community. I think if there is an equal amount of respect between teachers and principal—if the relationship is not one of fear—teachers will become involved in only those projects in which they are genuinely interested and that they care about; they will not be overinvolved, and everyone will benefit.

In the area of instructional leadership the mentor teacher can be trained to help the principal with new teachers. Having a mentor or teacher friend puts less pressure on novices, and mentors probably can be of more help because they are not seen as evaluators. I would hope the principal would give novice teachers more time than a few months or even one year to get their feet on the ground and begin to grow and learn as teachers, especially considering the inadequate number of education courses our novice teachers have had in their college preparation.

I agree it would be very beneficial for the principal to continue to be in the classroom as a teacher several times a year, but I can see realistically that this is increasingly hard to do because of demands on the principal for meetings, paperwork, observations, evaluations, and all the other required duties.

Regarding testing, I agree that this is a difficult challenge and that it is hard to draw the line as to how much emphasis is put on preparation for district, statewide, and national testing. I am glad this is not ultimately my responsibility. As a teacher I like to be supported with ideas, workshops, and interaction with my peers to develop strategies to help me better prepare my students for these tests.

I believe that the purpose of teacher evaluations is to help teachers grow professionally. I don't think that teacher evaluation should be used as a tool for control of administrators over teachers. If suggestions for improving professionally are communicated effectively and positively, then everyone will benefit— administrators, teachers, and most important the students.

The principals that I have worked with since the onset of the Time for Reflection project have sincerely tried to share decision making with their staff. I have seen in our site-based management training sessions how hard it is for the principals to give up their authority, mainly because they feel that they ultimately will be held responsible for the team's decisions and partly because of their personality, which led them to be principals in the first place. I hope as more and more people in our school are trained to reach decisions through shared decision making and consensus, there will be more trust that decisions will be made properly and will achieve what's best for the whole student population.

In closing, I would like to comment that I learned so much from the five dynamic university people about collaboration—about sharing ideas, about disagreeing but still respecting the other person's opinion, about compromising and not compromising. I learned, after fighting it all the way, that reflection is necessary for successful collaboration.

THE UNIVERSITY TEAM'S REFLECTIONS

The title of this chapter suggests that leadership in schools should be a shared process and that school leadership should not be limited solely to those who are designated as administrators. In Time for Reflection, school participants agreed to work together in collaborative teams, and Chapter 3 described the many accomplishments of those teams of teachers and principals. What we learned about school leadership through the formation and execution of each team's action plans is that there is more to the process than simply providing opportunities for leadership roles within the schools. Implementing shared leadership also requires the allocation of time, monies, and human resources to ensure that decisions can be implemented. Further, school leaders must have the flexibility to decide how best to use these resources. Shared leadership requires that district and school-level administrators be willing to take risks, as Gayle Holder pointed out. There must be a willingness to challenge the status quo and to accept mistakes as a normal part of decision making (Johnson, 1993b).

The meaning of collaborative leadership could be slightly different for each of the role groups represented. For the principal, collaborative leadership may mean sharing decisions with teachers through a process of site-based management that allows individuals to exercise their unique skills. For teacher leaders, collaborative leadership may imply equality among teachers and the ability to talk on equal terms with administrators, both building and districtwide. Teacher leaders may also define leadership in terms of their ability to share the role of instructional leader with administrators, as suggested by Jacqueline Hinojosa. And for novice teachers, collaborative leadership may mean serving as members of committees, spending time talking with other teachers in clusters or grade-level meetings, and having the ability to help make decisions that will improve learning conditions for their students. However one defines collaborative leadership, it is clear that in today's schools principals and teachers need each other and the unique skills and talents they bring to the schools. They need to be able to communicate and to feel free to express opinions about matters that concern their students. And they need to feel they can count on each other to ensure a positive learning environment for children.

CHAPTER 5

Novice Teachers: Mostly Action with No Support for Reflection

In Chapter 4, composites of a teacher leader and a principal were used to reveal the impact of Time for Reflection on two role groups. For school leaders, the effects were profound. In this chapter, we examine two other role groups who were targeted by four of the five leadership teams through projects designed to assist first-year teachers. Much of the data collection (both that of the leadership teams and that of the university staff) also focused on beginning teachers. The idea for locating these data within composite stories came from one of the elementary teachers we followed for 3 years. In our interactions with her, we always returned interview transcripts and fieldnotes for her verification. She called one of the university team members for a long discussion of one of the interviews and she asked what would be done with the data. The team member replied that the data would be analyzed and shared with the school leadership team and that, one day, it would be prepared for publication. She asked us to please protect her vulnerability and to remember that we had promised individual confidentiality. "I want my story told, but I don't want anyone to know it is me."

The following composites are representative of two groups of novice teachers: those who teach academic subjects and those who teach in special-subject areas such as physical education, art, music, or special education. It was deemed particularly important in the composite of the special-subject teacher not to specify a subject area, since those who teach the special subjects are usually the only ones in their schools to do so and specifying a subject would reveal the person's identity. The two novice composites are drawn from interviews and observations of 19 novice teachers who were teaching in the five TFR schools. Those interactions with novice teachers revealed that, while they had many problems in common, a different kind of alienation was experienced by special-subject teachers. Novices are often lumped into a single category in consideration of interventions, but we wanted to call attention to the needs of special-subject teachers because they are so different.

As in Chapter 4 each composite is followed by two commentaries, written by participants in TFR. These individuals are identified by their real names and job descriptions. The chapter ends with the university co-authors' analysis of lessons from the composites.

NOVICE ACADEMIC-SUBJECT TEACHER: A COMPOSITE STORY

I graduated from a small college in a southern state where I majored in English. I got married shortly after graduation, and my husband and I moved to a large city where he began a new job with a major oil company. I got a job in a large downtown office where I served as office manager. I worked in this job for a year and really hated it. It was so impersonal and tedious, that same routine day in and day out. I really felt like I needed more of a challenge. I needed to keep working for a while until my husband and I had paid off our student loans. I had taken two education courses in college and decided to see if I could become a teacher for the local urban school district.

Two weeks before school opened I applied for a job but was told there were no openings. Then a friend of mine told me that the way to get a job was to call the local principals directly and ask if they had any openings. I did this and found several middle schools that had openings in language arts and reading. The principals called the district personnel office, and I was called in to interview for a job as a reading teacher in a large middle school. I had never taken a course in how to teach reading, but the principal said that I could learn as I went and with my background in English it would not be difficult. I would have to take education courses since I would be hired on an emergency certificate. I contacted a local university and was told I would have to take an enormous amount of coursework at great expense in order to be certified. So I contacted another branch of this university a little further away and found that they required only half as many courses for certification. This made me really happy, since I knew it was going to be a real struggle to teach and go to school at the same time.

Because I was hired so close to the beginning of school, I missed the new teacher orientation and didn't get a lot of the information I needed about the routines and procedures at the school. I feel like I have been playing "catch-up" ever since. The other day, for instance, I was sick and didn't even know the procedure for calling in to get a substitute. I am still busy trying to figure out all the forms, slips, progress reports, and discipline referral paperwork.

When I arrived at the school for my first day of classes, I found I was to be a "floating" teacher. This meant that I have no permanent assigned classroom and must use other teachers' rooms during their conference period. I have six classes of reading improvement and I must transport all of my books and materials with me to different rooms all day. I have a large grocery cart that I can use, but since some of my classes are on the second floor, this presents a real problem in terms of logistics, especially if I want to show a video or filmstrip. And the first week of school, I wasn't given keys to all of the rooms, so I had to look for custodians to let me in.

One of the problems with using other teachers' rooms is that they have the rooms set up the way they want them, and they don't like me moving the furniture around, so this kind of limits the instructional techniques I can use. I also am not allowed to hang up my students' work on the walls, which is disappointing to me and them. Most of the teachers are pretty nice to me, but some seem really angry that I am intruding on "their" space.

Sometimes I get pretty depressed about the situation. I have six classes with as many as 33 students per class. These are all kids who are reading below grade level. Although they are supposed to be only one or two grade levels below, some in fact are almost nonreaders. I have no curriculum guide and very limited sets of classroom materials to use. Since I have never taught before and since I have never had a class in how to teach reading, my first year has been really tough. I really wish I had done student teaching so that I would have had some feel for what a teacher's day is like. I try to talk to some of the more experienced teachers to get ideas, but they are so busy with their own preparations, it is hard for them to spend much time with me except at cluster meetings. At those meetings we always have so much to do. We don't plan together, so most of the time I create my own lessons and develop my own materials. On the whole, while the teachers in the building are friendly, there is not much time to sit and visit or for me to pick their brains about what they are doing that is working in the classroom. Sometimes I talk to teachers in the copy room or lounge, but it would be nice to have more time to share. There must be some very experienced teachers in this school who could keep me from making many mistakes.

I am trying to find things that will be interesting for the kids. Some of the materials we have are either too babyish or don't relate to the culture of the students at all. I understand that each of the teachers in our department was allocated $300 to spend for materials and supplies, but our money was pooled before I got here and I had no input into the decision. The librarian has been very helpful in finding materials and classroom sets of books for me to use with my kids, but supplies are very limited. There are not enough materials to let students take things home. In most cases, there is only one classroom set.

Another new teacher and I have become good friends, and although she doesn't teach exactly the same classes as I do, we get together to share ideas and problems and to offer each other support. This interaction has been most valuable for me. I don't feel so alone here knowing that there is another person experiencing similar frustrations. However, with both of us being new, we are kind of floundering around for strategies that work. We are having fun, though, and we enjoy working together. Maybe someday we will even try to team teach a lesson.

I also was assigned to a mentor teacher here at the school. She has been very helpful to me and has tried to make me feel very welcome at the school. She teaches a different subject, however, so she can't help much with my lesson planning. She has given me some good ideas about how to deal with kids and has told me a little bit about the community and the school.

I rarely see the principal of our school. He seems so busy that I hate to bother him with my problems. I'm not sure he even knows who I am. He seems to be doing a good job of running this large school, however. He is new to the building this year and maybe he is feeling as overwhelmed as I am. Sometimes the area superintendent comes to visit the school. When the students were threatening a walkout one day, the area superintendent came and set up a command post in the school. There was a lot of excitement for a while, but nothing ever materialized.

The dean of students is very nice and, if I can catch him in the hallway to ask him for something, he always comes through for me. But he and the assistant principals are all so busy dealing with students that it's difficult for them to find time to help new teachers. It is their job to evaluate me as a teacher, however. They come in and observe for an hour and fill out an evaluation form. They don't get a complete picture of me as a classroom teacher from these limited visits. I am the one who is with these kids all day, every day, and I really kind of resent someone coming in for a one-shot evaluation. I guess that is their job, but it really makes me angry sometimes when I get marked low in one category or another.

One thing that has been helpful this year has been the seminars for first-year teachers offered one Saturday a month by the district and the university. At first I thought, "Oh, no, I am working 10 hours a day, 5 days a week just to keep afloat and now they want me to go on Saturdays, too!" But the sessions have turned out to be very helpful for me and have addressed a lot of the areas I was having difficulty with—like lesson planning, which no one ever showed me how to do, and classroom management, which is a real challenge for me, especially with the large classes I have to teach. I was afraid these sessions would be too theoretical, like the education classes I took in college, but they have really been very practical. This is one program that definitely should be continued. Some of the other district-mandated inservices have been of little value and are basically a waste of time. I would rather have the free time to work in my classroom than to have to sit through boring meetings. But we don't have a choice.

A surprise about teaching has been how exhausting it is. I come home from school and collapse on the couch until dinnertime. Then I get up and make dinner, grade papers, and prepare for the next day's classes. I never really appreciated how hard teachers had to work and how little rest there is during the day. It seems like the day zooms by. We are with the kids all day except for our planning period and lunch. (Thank goodness the state has mandated duty-free lunch, or we'd have to eat with the kids, too.) Sometimes I eat with my students just for fun because I enjoy being with them and they seem to enjoy my company. I understand that in some schools teachers have aides to help them, but here we are pretty much on our own. We can get things duplicated by the office aides, but the turnaround time is pretty long and I don't ever seem to be able to plan that far in advance, so I end up doing all my own copying. That can be pretty time-consuming, since I have so few textbooks or workbooks that are usable. And the copier is so old and of such poor quality. Materials and supplies are almost nonexistent here.

The first few weeks of school, I heard about a Danforth Foundation project that our school was involved in. I really don't understand what this project is all about. One of the teachers asked me if I would be interested in joining the team, but I said no. I am so overwhelmed by everything here, that I can't afford to give any energy to meetings and retreats. If it is not something that will directly help me in my classroom tomorrow, I'm just not interested at this point. The teachers who are involved in the project seem to be enjoying it. They have monthly potato luncheons for us and they sponsored a nice back-to-school breakfast. I guess they also helped set up the inservice we had at the beginning of second semester. That was a lot of fun and the teachers really got to know each other better. This is such a large school that it is easy to get lost as a teacher. The Danforth team also started an evening tutoring program for parents and students, and teachers to take turns volunteering to work there. So far, the turnout is low, but the people who come return each week. The mothers are starting to cook food for the sessions, and attendance is slowly increasing. Little brothers, sisters, and even some high school students have started coming over for help. Maybe this is a start in the right direction. It is difficult to stay for tutoring when you are so exhausted at the end of the day, but I volunteer my time when I can. Maybe when I am a more experienced teacher, I will find out more about this group and participate in it. Right now, I am just trying to survive!

The Students. I guess what really surprised me the most as a new teacher was the lives of the students. I grew up in a middle-class environment in a small town and I guess I never really thought about poverty that much. These kids here are so poor and have so little that it really blew me away. Things that I take for granted are luxuries to them. Many of them come from very abusive homes as well, where there is drinking and drugs and violence. In addition, they are abused by the police in the neighborhood. It is so sad that sometimes when I hear their stories I can't help but cry. How can we expect them to come to school and learn when they are dealing with all this disruption in their personal and home lives? It frustrates me to feel so helpless. Many of them have never even been downtown. And they have no idea where the university is or even what it is. There is no connection in their minds between education and success in life.

It is hard for me to overcome those odds in my classroom. I have referred a number of students for counseling or diagnostic testing, but nothing seems to happen. I guess there is a big backlog of cases. Every time I try to refer, I must fill out a ton of paperwork. After going through all that and then have nothing happen, one gets discouraged. Meanwhile, however, I am trying to conduct classes where there are several very disturbed and disruptive students. I know they need help, but until they get it, I am stuck trying to deal with problems I have no training to deal with. The other day in our cluster meeting, we heard that one of our most troublesome students was transferring to another school, and we all cheered! I know that might seem like a terrible attitude for teachers to have, but we really did all that we could for him and he was totally disrupting our classes. I wish there were some solutions to these kinds of problems.

Classroom management has really been a major problem for me. It was very difficult for me to keep kids on-task at first. There was a lot of talking, out-of-seat behavior, arguing, and sleeping. I was really feeling overwhelmed. I had never received any training in this area. I tried to ask other teachers what they did to manage their classes, but none of the suggestions they gave me seemed to make an impact. Finally, someone gave a workshop on classroom management at our Saturday workshops. I got some ideas and the names of some books to read. One of the most important things I learned was that the lesson needs to be fast-paced and interesting to keep kids on-task. Also, that students learn best in different ways. Most of my kids are very verbal and social and hate reading a text or doing worksheets. When I started to vary the activities a little, they became more responsive. That was difficult to do, however, since I had never had a teaching methods class. So I experimented and learned by trial and error.

The general expectation here seems to be to keep your students in their seats and quiet and not send kids down to the office. But there are times when the kids and I are having so much fun with a learning activity that it does get a little noisy. And they need to keep active. Their attention spans are short, and I have to vary the activities for them frequently. I think I should be the one to decide how noisy the classroom needs to be, as long as we are not disrupting others in the building.

What really amazes me is how great most of these kids are in spite of their environment and their poverty. I really love most of them. They are so eager to learn and offer to help me in the classroom. I really love to read, and I am trying to instill that love in my students. Just sitting there doing worksheets is definitely not the answer. Now that I am getting a little more comfortable with my teaching and management skills, I have been trying out some new techniques with them, like cooperative group work and projects, puzzles, and games.

One of my students is really an excellent poet. I accidentally saw a poem he had written, and it was really good. I am encouraging him to do more of that. Another boy who is almost a nonreader is a terrific artist. I am getting him to illustrate stories and then I help him write the words. I think his reading skills are really growing. These kids really grab your heart. I am very glad that I am teaching here instead of some upper-middle-class school. Here at least I feel that the students really need me. I can watch their progress and know that I had some responsibility for it. It is hard not to be discouraged by the kids I can't reach, however. The experienced teachers tell me we all have to accept the fact that some kids have problems that are so overwhelming that we can't help them. That's hard for me to accept. I can understand why inner-city teachers "burn out" after a few years. It is really frustrating to be teaching what you think is an exciting concept or lesson and see that there are students with their heads down on their desks. I tend to take that very personally, like I have failed to inspire them.

One interesting thing about middle school kids and kids from this culture in particular is how important the peer group is to them. They really stick together and defend one another. Their social lives are more important than anything else. Sometimes these relationships can be disruptive in the classroom, but I am learning how to channel them in positive directions. For example, we are starting to do some drama in the classroom and they love acting out stories. My only problem is trying to deal with their behavior to keep it from becoming too disruptive as they get carried away with the activity. I am even trying to start a drama club. These kids need to have the same opportunities that kids in the middle-class schools have. My friend and I are sponsoring the cheerleaders this year, and that has been a wonderful experience for us. The girls are so grateful for our help and so excited about being cheerleaders.

The Cluster System. The only teachers I really know well are those in my cluster. I like the cluster system a lot. At our school, the kids are divided into groups of 150 and have the same six teachers all day. We teachers all have the same planning period, and we meet to discuss the kids and their needs. We also use this time for parent conferences. It is really difficult to get the parents involved in their children's education at this school. I know that part of the problem is the language barrier, but it also may have something to do with the fact that many of these parents have little schooling themselves. They don't understand the value of school for their kids. It would be helpful if we had a translator with us during our conferences. Now, the students do the translating, and who knows how much they are telling their parents! I heard that one cluster team was taking a course in conversational Spanish so that they could better communicate with parents. That's a great idea, but I don't know where I would find time to do that with all the other courses I am required to take for certification. I know that some of the parents really do want to help, but it is so difficult to tell them how to do it. They must have very difficult lives themselves, and there is not much time or energy left over to deal with school problems.

My cluster team has helped me through some rough spots this year. We are really becoming like a family. It is helpful to have five other teachers who have the same students you do. You can plan consistent programs to help them and also to work with their families. We have some great discussions at our meetings. The teachers have helped me a lot with grading and the forms I need to fill out.

One of them took the time to show me how to organize my time and materials a little more effectively. I hope that we continue to use this system next year. It's a great benefit for a beginning teacher, and I think that it really helps the kids a lot, too. It's hard to get help in a school with over 2,000 students. At least here, they are part of a little family and get to know each other and us well. Maybe that will help motivate some of them to come to school more often. Absenteeism has been a big problem here, as has been the turnover rate. It's discouraging to have worked hard with a student and then find out that he or she has checked out of school!

This first year of teaching has been rough, but also very rewarding in a number of ways. I found that my knowledge of English did not give me sufficient preparation to teach reading. And my lack of education courses really did hurt me in the classroom. I am looking forward to taking some methods courses this summer and am already starting to plan with my friend the new and creative ways we are going to try to reach our kids next year. We'd like to take them on some field trips to broaden their horizons and show them the world outside of the neighborhood. We'll need to find some funding for that, but I am sure we will be able to. So I'll be back next year. My first year here has been both painful and rewarding. One thing, though—it has convinced me that I made the right choice to become a teacher. It certainly has never been boring or routine and the rewards can't be duplicated—the look on a student's face when he or she understands a concept, the note or gift from a grateful student, or the tears in a mother's eyes when you tell her how well her child is doing. Teaching is not a career for the faint of heart, and there are lots of discouragements along the way. There are lots of things that schools and districts could do to make teaching easier. But I'm going to stay in it. Hopefully, each year I'll become a little better at what I do.

A Math Teacher's Commentary

The first commentary was written by Becky Gill, a middle school English-as-a-Second-Language (ESL) math teacher. As a 3-year member of Broadstreet's leadership team, Becky was very involved in the evening tutoring program.

The story of this novice teacher or any novice teacher is a very emotional topic for me. I feel that the first few years of teaching are made incredibly difficult by the system and by the new teacher herself. As a result what should be the beginning of a career in education becomes an experience that drives a person away from teaching. Without guidance and help many teachers will never experience success.

I remember my first years of teaching as a continual struggle. I guess 13 years in public schools and 4 years in college did not prepare me to be in control of a classroom. I knew from the beginning of my first year that I needed help with many aspects of teaching. But I was very insecure and did not want others to think

I wasn't doing my job. No one came to me to offer help so eventually I went looking for it. I found most experienced teachers thought problems could be handled easily with only one or two techniques. Others said it was personal preference, whatever worked for the individual.

I did receive help from some teachers, but they were not in my field. Therefore they could help only on general classroom routines. This did help me enormously but still left a lot of gaps in the specific lessons. Since that time I have wondered why I could not find an experienced math teacher to help me. There are many possibilities but I'm sure my own insecurity had a lot to do with it. I did not want others to know I was not succeeding. Now as an experienced teacher I see that young teachers can be intimidated. Maybe that was part of the problem.

Like the teacher in this study, my greatest resource was another first-year teacher who had alternative certification. We talked *a lot* about what worked and what didn't. We tried a lot of different things. I had heard the first year would be difficult and knew I would have a lot of disappointments. But I never knew how difficult it would be. Even now as an experienced teacher I cannot forget those terrible years as a new teacher. I guess that is why I feel it is very important to develop relationships with new teachers at my school. I try to make myself available to offer support in any way I can, even informally.

Many districts now have begun mentoring programs for all new teachers. This program gives new teachers the resource of an experienced teacher in their subject area. I believe this is one of the best ways you can improve the chances for a new teacher. A good mentor should be able to help a new teacher with those aspects of the job that are the most discouraging. There are so many questions that a new teacher has, and a mentor can help reassure her. I also feel it is very important that the mentor is in the same field to help with the actual lessons and techniques.

I'm not sure what a principal's role in nurturing a new teacher should be. After years of teaching I do know that evaluation is a minor part of the principal's role. As a new teacher, my perception of the principal was "boss." I looked to him to help me and tell me how I was doing. He did not see the importance of nurturing new teachers in both positive and negative ways. He gave only positive strokes, which were necessary but not helpful. He enabled me to keep going because he seemed to think I was successful, but he never really knew what the atmosphere of my classroom was like. Sometimes survival is all that's important in the inner city. The actual amount of effective learning time is not.

These feelings continue into my evaluations. I was happy with an average evaluation even when I disagreed with the specifics. But I knew it was not a real reflection of my teaching, my abilities, or my successes. If they had been a fly on the wall every day they would never have given me such a good evaluation. I truly believe the evaluations were a reflection more of my desire to be successful and to be a good teacher than of my actual success.

During my novice years I believed that the basic math concepts were the most important thing. No matter how much difficulty I had with school policy or lesson plans, I would spend every day trying to explain math. You know—follow the book, teach page 1, then page 2, then page 3. I never finished the book. I soon realized math couldn't be taught without classroom control so I continued to try new ideas—but still focused on math—boring lessons, but math. It was several years before I got to the fun part. Now I know it has to be interesting before they'll learn. Even though in my first year I knew these kids were from a place I couldn't relate to, I was so wrapped up in my need to succeed that I didn't see some of the needs of the students. I also didn't consider that in my approach—-again it would have been nice if someone had told me.

Feeling needed! After fighting my way to a semi-successful classroom, I was overcome with this feeling. Even if I wasn't the best teacher, I was making a difference for a few kids. It made me feel great—that's one advantage of teaching in an inner city. I never had that feeling in small town white America.

I'd have never made it through my first year in the English-as-a-Second-Language area without my great cluster team. I took a big risk by changing subject areas, but it was the best thing I could have done. Learning, experience, and a chance to feel successful. Those things make all the difference.

A Reading Teacher's Commentary

Ernie Ortiz, a middle school teacher with 19 years of experience, wrote the second commentary. As a member of Broadstreet's leadership team, he was active in all of the projects over the 3 years of the project. After TFR ended, he transferred to another middle school where he is currently involved in the district's innovative attempt to establish curriculum for a new technology-centered K–8 school.

"You'll never get there if you don't know where you're going." I take this to mean that unless you have a purpose for a journey you should put it off until you come up with an itinerary. I think the same applies to the students we encounter in the middle grades. I remember one student in particular walking behind me during passing periods to class. He would always ask, "Why do you walk so fast?" and every time I would reply, "I'm not walking fast. I have someplace to go, and I need to get there."

Novice teachers are forced to come to terms with changes in their lives, and at the same time deal with the changes in their students' lives. Many of the students we deal with in our first year, and every year after that, have no purpose in life other than to survive moment to moment. And they are in no hurry to begin any task. The reason that the first year is so hard for teachers is that we tend to forget that not everyone is operating on our agenda. The new teacher has achieved his or her purpose: to become a teacher. Doesn't everyone operate on the same wavelength?

Universities are notorious for creating false environments in relation to teaching. One local university has its education students teach in a laboratory-type setting there on campus. Talk about misguided! While some other universities are better, still the future teacher is told to expect potential problems with inadequate homelife, troubled neighborhoods, drugs, and so forth. If I was told that the students I was trying to teach were neglected and underprivileged, my inclination would be to help them. But the best way to help these students is to educate them— period. As they become educated, they can be helped emotionally and physically.

A new teacher has a double dilemma. How do you come across as an authority figure for your students? How do you present a competent face to your colleagues? There have been various programs to improve teaching, and veteran teachers have made concerted efforts to make the novice teachers more comfortable. The first year of the Danforth project at my school, there were 10 or 12 novice teachers. Many of them were completely lost unless some veteran recognized a need to help. This problem was corrected the second year of the project when "buddies" were assigned to the new teachers. The new teachers were more involved and better focused toward all areas.

Probably the most important concept for new teachers is to create environments that have decided structures for each of the students. This does not mean the teacher has to focus individually on the students, but rather a base for learning is presented to the whole. When the students that need individual instruction begin to emerge, the class has the basis on which to continue with minimal direction. All this comes to mind from reading the novice teacher's concern about her low level/nonreader students. If you try to focus on one or two students in order to save them, without preparing for the whole group, you lose everyone.

Administrators have always been open to well-designed requests for materials, monies, time. New teachers should recognize that these are parameters in which they can operate with minimal concern for the blessings of administration. The saying that it is easier to ask forgiveness than it is to ask permission comes to mind. Somehow new teachers need to feel empowered.

NOVICE SPECIAL-SUBJECT TEACHER: A COMPOSITE STORY

This story is being written as a part of the Time for Reflection project in which my school participated, but in which I played only a small part as an interviewee. I have been aware of the activities of the leadership team in my school, especially when they provided lunches or special programs for the new teachers, but otherwise the project did not really have much of an influence on my teaching or on what I see of the school activities. However, I do realize, because of questions asked by the interviewer from the university, that a focus of the project was on collaborative work within the school. So in my story I will discuss my relationships with administrators and other teachers, and the way those relationships affected how I learned to teach during my first 3 years and on into what is now my fourth year of teaching. In the last part of the story, I will talk about learning to teach in the particular kind of isolation that belongs to those in the school who traditionally have been marginalized, not out of meanness, but simply out of benign neglect.

The first thing I want to address is the question, "What does it mean to be a teacher?" Some people might laugh at that question, but to me it is at the heart of my struggle to be accepted in my school both as a knowledgeable professional and as a colleague by other teachers and administrators. My story is about how I am learning to teach alone when it appears that all around me other teachers have companionship and help from other, more experienced teachers that they need to be successful, even in their first year of teaching. From the title of the project, I understand that the leadership team was attempting to find ways of increasing teachers' opportunities to reflect together about their teaching. I remember hearing about reflection during my college preparation, and I'll talk more later about what reflection means to me.

My story is also about my struggle for acceptance from my colleagues, students, and parents at a time when educators and the public seem to be concerned only about standardized test scores. In the special-subject areas such as art, music, and physical education, standardized tests are not used as a measure of achievement, so some people consider those subjects less important than reading, writing, and the other basics. But those of us who teach the special subjects consider them just as important as academics to the education of children. In fact, for some children they represent the part of the day that is most rewarding and exciting. As you will see in the next sections, I don't have to convince my administrators of the importance of the special subjects; when it comes to support, I know I can count on them.

Relationships with Administrators. My school is a great school, but only because all of the teachers and administrators work so hard to make it so. The principal is recognized throughout the district for her ability to create an atmosphere for learning in our building, and I'm very proud to work with her. She is also a caring person who knows the name of almost every child. In my first month of teaching, I naively asked her to informally visit one of my classes to see if she could give me some pointers on management and discipline, but she never found the time, even though I know she wanted to visit my class. I understand better now that she has so many demands on her time and often has to be out of the building to attend meetings at central administration. When she is in the building, she keeps an open-door policy, and I feel confident that if I talked to her about a problem, she would listen and try to help me. Since my first year of teaching, I've realized that even though the principal is called the school's instructional leader, she can't possibly be expected to help all the beginning and experienced teachers with their problems. I did receive some help from the assistant principal, who has more time to talk with teachers. But my interactions with the administrators have been primarily during the times when they come into my class to conduct the twice yearly evaluations. The tension in the building is almost palpable during evaluations, but the principal does everything she can to make the experience nonthreatening. All of the teachers are very grateful when it's over.

My teaching evaluations have been excellent, but I have been concerned since my first year of teaching about what I have to do to get a good evaluation. In fact, I call the evaluation lesson my "dog and pony show." The evaluators look for a lesson with all the elements that have been identified on the evaluation instrument, including a verbal instructional input portion. However, in the special subjects where a good lesson should provide lots of practice time for children, the traditional type of lesson may not be appropriate. To prepare for the evaluations, I've begun using visual aids during the instructional input part of many of my lessons. Sometimes I make a poster or bulletin board and use information from that to supplement my lecture on rules, safety, or a new skill. But I feel torn between what I believe is good for children, which is more activity time, and what the evaluation instrument forces me to do, which is talk to them more. It seems very unfair to evaluate all teachers with the same instrument. One of the things I learned during my first 2 years is that you can't just introduce the special lesson cycle on evaluation days and have a successful lesson. Instead, you have to teach your routines to the children so that when the evaluation does come, it's just like any other day. What this means is that many of my lessons include lectures that take from 10 to 15 minutes of time away from the activity.

Regardless of my reservations about how evaluation of teaching is done, I would have to say the evaluation instrument has changed the way I teach. For example, I often use posters and actually write out the major points that are covered in the lesson. At first that seemed like a lot of work, but now I really like having it up all the time, and it seems to help the children understand what I want them to do. I consider the evaluation itself as just another of the many hurdles that the state places in front of teachers—a necessary evil but something that was not very helpful to me in learning to teach.

I mentioned in the beginning that my story is about learning to teach without the support of other, more experienced teachers, but this applies also to administrators. Very often a week goes by without my even seeing the principal, if we don't have a faculty meeting. The assistant principal also has been one of my evaluators some years, but there is a different relationship there, probably because I see him more often than I see the principal. Maybe because the assistant principal is able to spend more time with the teachers, some feel they can talk more easily to him about personal as well as school problems. He has been very helpful on many occasions when I've had to deal with angry parents or other teachers, and I really value the way he always backs me up. If there's a question from a parent about what I have done, he is always there to calm the situation and help explain how we do things at the school.

While I'm talking about administrators, I should mention my district coordinator, who coordinates programs in my subject area between schools. He also serves on evaluation teams. When he was my evaluator, I was very nervous because he has such different ideas about good teaching than I do. I was forced to be a very stern disciplinarian and keep my students quiet when he was observing. Once, when I had to be out of school, the coordinator substituted for me for a day. The next day when I got back, my students and other teachers told me how much trouble he had teaching my classes. That made me feel very good about myself to know that I can manage the kids who gave him such a hard time.

One of the good things he does for us is arrange for new teachers to observe a special-subject teacher in another school. When I first heard about the visits, I was afraid that if you were sent to observe another teacher it meant that you weren't doing a good job, but then I realized that all the new teachers were doing it, so I didn't mind. Many of my ideas about management and discipline came from that one day when I visited two other schools. The coordinator also organizes idea exchange nights once a month, and teachers bring their best ideas to share.

I've learned so much about organization from the idea exchanges. The other good thing about the idea sharing is that it gives me contact once a month with other teachers from my subject area. While on the one hand I enjoy the sharing of ideas with colleagues once a month, that experience always serves to remind me of how lonely school can be for special-subject teachers. I don't mean lonely in the sense that I never see other teachers, but I mean that there is no one else who teaches my subject. Other teachers are able to offer moral support and give advice, but they don't really know my subject.

Relationships with Other Teachers. Other teachers have been a great help to me in learning how they handle behavior problems, and I've tried to make my behavior management system consistent with theirs. This is important because the children respond better if they are treated consistently during the day. For me, this means that I need to know how every single teacher handles discipline. The biggest challenge was figuring out a system for handling the paperwork so all the behavior problems were documented and then reported to the classroom teachers. Report cards, which contain grades for all the subject areas, are filled out by the classroom teacher. Therefore, the communication has to be good during the grading period and when it comes time to assign grades. This isn't easy when you remember that I teach every child in the school every week, whereas the academic teachers usually work only with a couple of classes in the upper grades and only 22 students in the lower grades. Now, after 3 years, I've finally figured out a system that is working. I document every word and every misbehavior so that if a child received an unsatisfactory mark from me, there is evidence to back it up.

Of all the people in the school, I've noticed that only the cafeteria aide has problems similar to mine. For instance, we both manage large groups of children at one time. I noticed that when she lines up the children, she calls on one table at a time. That idea was really helpful to me, and I found it works well in my class too. She also has to manage the children as they move around the cafeteria getting their trays and returning them after lunch. Similarly in my classroom, the children are not always sitting in one place the whole period as they use various pieces of equipment. Just being aware of how she manages all the children at once has been helpful to me.

Now that I've taught a few years, most of the procedures at my school seem simple. But the first few years, I often wished that someone would sit down with me and explain how things work. For example, I remember thinking in the beginning that when students were walking down the hall, they were required to stop at every clock. Of course, now I realize that the teachers just use the clocks as a sort of marker, but as a new teacher I didn't understand the difference between formal rules and simple procedures that everyone uses because they are helpful. My first experience with other teachers in the building came my first year when I was assigned to a buddy teacher from third grade. Once when I was having problems getting some of my classes lined up at the end of the period, she suggested that I reward them with candy. What she didn't realize is that I would be buying candy for 650 children since I teach every child in the school in a week. After this experience I realized that other teachers would not be able to understand my situation since they work with a smaller group of students all day long. They don't know how hard it is to learn the names of all the students in school during the first few weeks of the term. Other teachers don't seem aware that I teach two classes at a time while they teach single classes.

One continuing problem I've encountered with other teachers happens on a regular basis at the beginning and end of classes. Sometimes, if I don't allow enough time for students to calm down at the end of class, I find myself lining up my 50 students while, at the same time, the next 50 students are already entering my classroom. The classroom teachers complain about how difficult it is to control their 25 children, so you would expect them to be more understanding about the difficulty of controlling 50 at a time. But some don't seem aware that it's a problem. Because I'm a special-subject teacher, I can handle it. Even after I ask as courteously as I can that teachers hold their classes until the previous one leaves, some of them are in such a hurry to begin their conference period that they just leave the children. I wish they would remember that my class isn't just their conference period—it's a real class just like their own.

After my first year, I made up my mind that when the classroom teachers come to my class, their students will be lined up and quiet. This decision was based on the fact that the teachers in this school put so much emphasis on having children quiet and orderly at all times. I disagree with this for special subjects, but this expectation is so strong in my school that I have to follow it. I start with very firm expectations and rules for how to enter and leave the room, and every child knows where to sit when they enter the room. If they come in too noisily, they just have to go out and do it over. I stop 5 minutes before the end of the period to get the children lined up and quiet. Then we talk quietly and review important parts of the lesson or prepare for the next day. This has made a big difference in comments I get from other teachers. I learned the hard way that you have to do things in your classroom the same way every day, whether you feel like it or not. Now I think the other teachers perceive me as a real teacher, but it's too bad that their opinion is based on the beginning and end of the class period rather than on what goes on during the period.

One of the things that I have had to learn is how to get along with lots of different people. As a special-subject teacher, I work with every person in the school at some time and it's important to me to have a good working relationship with everyone. As a beginning teacher, I assumed that other teachers would just automatically treat me as a fellow professional, but in my first year I found that doesn't necessarily happen. For example, one day I was walking down the hall talking to another teacher about an incident that happened with a parent. A teacher happened to overhear part of the conversation and misunderstood what I said. She confronted me in the lounge in front of other teachers, but I was so surprised by this that I couldn't even answer—I only felt embarrassed as I stammered for an answer. The experience left me a little bitter but also surprised that this could happen with a colleague.

Being the Only One in My Subject. Sometimes I feel jealous of teachers in the grade-level areas where they always have other teachers around them to offer advice and materials. Not only am I the only teacher in my subject area, but also I'm physically located outside of the main building. Unless I go to the teachers' lounge during my conference period, I can go through a whole day and not see another adult except when teachers bring their classes to me. But going to the lounge has its drawbacks. For example, going to the lounge means not being able to work on grading or lessons because just as soon as I start talking with another teacher, we get into a conversation about some student and before I know it the period is over. These conversations are sometimes very helpful in understanding a child's problems in the classroom, but other things don't get done. The academic teachers can share materials and lesson plans with others in their grade level or subject, and I imagine that they must talk during the day about how their lessons are going. But there's no one in the school who can help me think about a particular lesson and how it could be changed or improved. To me that's what reflection is all about. But it's hard to reflect alone. Basically I have had to learn from experience, which means I have learned lots of lessons the hard way. It would mean a lot to be able to watch other teachers on a regular basis, but it seems that is something reserved for first-year teachers only. There was one interesting activity that was organized by my school's leadership team. One day each semester, teachers could sign up to spend half a day visiting other teachers' classes. I signed up the first time and really enjoyed seeing how the classroom teachers interact with the children. The only problem was that no one came to visit my classroom that day. I think next time I'll invite several teachers to come because I'd really like them to see what we do and how the children learn in my class.

All of the special-subject teachers in my school meet together once a week, but our meetings are related only to announcements from the administrators. Since we all teach different subjects, we really have little in common. We occasionally talk about problems with certain students, but often our meeting time is taken up with talk about schedules or special programs. One of the things that would help me most is having time at least once a week to talk about the students with their classroom teachers. When the classroom teacher has a problem with a student, there are always other teachers around to watch the class or to help with the problem. If I have a problem, I have to either send the student to the office by himself or take him and leave my class alone. I teach the children in this school every year, and there are some things I know about the students that might be helpful to their teachers. I feel that I know the children better in some ways than their classroom teachers know them. On the other hand, the classroom teachers know things about the students that I don't know—especially about their home lives. If we had a chance to share our knowledge, I think the students would benefit, and I could be more understanding about the ways children act out their frustrations with each other in my class. The academic teachers work in grade-level teams that meet weekly, but there is no formal way for the special-subject teachers to meet with them since we teach their students while they have planning time. If I want to know about a particular student, I have to catch the teacher before or after school or in the hall between classes. I don't think this kind of information sharing is a very satisfactory way to help children.

Concluding Words. I've tried to present a balanced picture of what it's been like during my beginning years of teaching; that is, I've talked about the pluses and the minuses. All in all, my first 3 years have been a good experience. There are some things I would like to change if I could go back and do them over or if I had the power to change them, but I would definitely not change my school or my decision to be a special-subject teacher.

In my story, I've tried to make a strong case for everyone in the school being part of the growth experiences that sometimes are planned just for academic teachers. I've tried to show that everyone will benefit from including the special-subject teachers in every aspect of the school. My suggestion is to look for things that all teachers have in common, like the children, discipline and management problems, and the need to grow professionally. My idea is that if all teachers in the school are committed to professional growth and continual learning, then the students will naturally adopt a similar frame of mind. I think I'm being heard because my school is taking a leadership role in planning a program for new teachers.

A Special-Subject Teacher's Commentary

Janis Young, a special education teacher, wrote the first commentary. During the project, Janis taught at Woods Elementary school where she was active in both RITE and the leadership team's projects. After transferring to an elementary school closer to her home, she became involved in her new district's innovative programs in special education. She reports that because of TFR, she is now a much more as-sertive school leader.

The character strengths described in this teacher were realistic. A special-subject teacher must be flexible. Her traits are similar to those found in elementary school teachers across America. The ability to be flexible and adaptable are traits that make special-subject programs work. By their very nature, these classes support instruction. Hence, classroom teachers sometimes view them as supplemental rather than core classes. I could relate to her feelings of uncertainty. I do not believe that anyone has taken the time to explain the inner workings of a school to me. I make deductions constantly but I'm not sure if these deductions are valid. I have allowed time and observation to be the litmus test for reality.

The special-subject teacher was on target when she said that the objectives taught in her class are not those generally tested on standardized tests. Perhaps this is why her curriculum is considered isolated from the regular classroom. Perhaps this is why she felt isolated.

What happened to this special-subject teacher during her first instructional years is unfortunate but true. I can relate to her frustrations. I was in such dire need of direction that I resigned after teaching for a year and a half. I opted to stay home with my new child. I cited the inconsistencies of administrators as one reason for my resignation. I was fresh out of college and I wanted someone to tell me what to do. I felt that if I knew the rules I would be sure to follow them. I was disappointed to find that rules were ever changing and interpretations varied from personality to personality.

Economically, I could not live with my decision to leave the classroom. I returned to teaching and found myself in a very unfavorable situation. I was working for a female principal who was concerned more with being politically correct than with doing what was best for kids. I managed to finish my year with her and her department chairperson, who just did her paperwork correctly and kept the kids quiet. Luckily for me, another principal approved my transfer. I was surprised with the difference I noticed from one building to the next. First of all, this new principal was very confident. She had worked at several enterprises before becoming a principal and she had worked outside of education.

The one thing I remember most about this new principal was her belief that her campus could be beautiful. She took an inner-city school and transferred it into a beautiful flower garden. The landscaping was outstanding. She promoted getting the kids outside long before the district reinstated recess periods. Birds live on our school grounds. I grew under this principal. She handpicked her special-subject teachers, and she assigned an experienced teacher to help me. The principal was old enough to be my mother. She showed me a lot of shortcuts. She was happy in her job, and I became happy in my job too. I never felt threatened. I could have remained in that school until I retired if it were not for the 60-mile round trip commute daily. So, after 3 years, I took a chance and transferred to a school close to home.

I was a lot wiser than I was on my initial re-entry into teaching. I had attended workshops to ask other teachers if they had vacancies on their campuses. I asked about their principals. I had learned by then that if the principal is good, the teachers know it. I had heard a lot of good things about my new principal. She had heard a lot of good things about me. In fact, she approved my transfer based on recommendations she received prior to meeting me. The new principal was great, but the climate of the school wasn't as great as I anticipated. I encountered problems similar to those in the special-subject teacher composite. Like her I found myself crying out for help but not knowing whom to ask. I wasn't sure if I was aware of the importance of asking. I sometimes choose to keep silent rather than face the consequences of speaking up.

The teachers were all about my age, and there was a lot of competition for recognition. This competition was the source of most of my problems. Working collaboratively was difficult because everyone wanted to shine. Looking back though, I think I understand why we encountered difficulties. The principal simply recruited well and she had a lot of qualified personnel on her campus. As in the case of the special-subject teacher, my principal was very supportive. She solicited my expertise on instructional matters. I was allowed the opportunity to grow professionally and to contribute to instructional goals for the school.

Similar to the special-subject teacher in this composite, my peers did not understand my job. They felt that because my classes were small my job was easy. They simply did not care that I taught several levels and lesson planning was a time-consuming task. My students were not always motivated, and I spent a great deal of my instructional efforts on motivational activities. This gave them the perception that I spent a lot of time playing rather than teaching. My problem was one of teacher perception. Is it the job of the special-subject teacher to define her role to classroom teachers? Undeniably, I share a responsibility for perceptions held by others.

This forces me to look at the consequences of keeping silent. Keeping silent perpetuates the existing situations that we do not like. Should teachers help themselves? Is it important to change perceptions held by other teachers? Can the principal improve teacher perceptions of roles within the school? What do principals communicate as important? The fact that this teacher had to teach twice as many students in an hour seemed to suggest that her job is a lesser job. This seems to communicate to regular classroom teachers that her job is easier than theirs. Is it perception that builds a type of resentment that the special-subject teacher gets paid the same salary for less work? Is it this resentment and lack of knowledge that breed uncomfortable school climates? This is ironic because like the teacher in this story, I feel that my work is not valued. My contribution to the staff is questioned by my peers. I resent that.

The teacher in this composite seemed happy in her job. She seemed confident in her ability to survive in a less than positive climate. Considering her job description might shed light on her role. Did her job description suggest that she was to teach music or art independently of the regular program? As a special-subject teacher I have learned that my subject is a critical component of the educational system. I do see my role as changing. Instead of planning separately, I need to plan collaboratively with the classroom teacher. Perhaps I could build or support an integrated lesson.

Integrated learning is one area in which a special-subject teacher can contribute and support the classroom teacher and feel more involved in the academic process. As a special-subject teacher I feel that I would benefit from inclusion at grade-level meetings. The isolation of the special-subject teacher will continue as long as she allows it to continue. It will continue as long as administrators and classroom teachers allow it to continue. The special-subject teacher, like many others, can do much to change her role if she is given time for collaboration and planning. Perhaps campus goals could include and redefine her role as a support to education. The special-subject teacher can do much to improve her situation if she is given a format and a time in which to do so.

The best skill I learned as a leadership team member during this project was getting the teachers to collaborate—to share their vast knowledge and develop a consensus. We found that our ideas about discipline were similar. We developed a plan to improve discipline in the hallways. The principal did not participate in the process. The teachers were free to speak openly and honestly. The competition was channeled in a positive manner. The collaboration and connection between special subjects and the classroom should be strengthened, thereby adding to the cost effectiveness and efficiency of having these programs in elementary schools.

Am I responsible for developing a format for change? Why should I? Can I? There is a reluctance to challenge the status quo. How assertive is too assertive? Within schools, there are too many opportunities to regret being assertive. There are too many climates and too many repercussions that breed within the cultures of schools. I don't worry about changing perceptions as much as I worry about communicating truth. I would appreciate the continued inclusion of my role in supporting campus goals. I work hard teaching and planning. My job may not be viewed as number one on campus. But it is a number. It has a place and a function on our campus. The project, Time for Reflection, has allowed me to come to closure about my role. It has given me the courage to change some things I would not have addressed otherwise. I look forward to the promises of school restructuring and change. Whether special-subject or regular classroom teacher, we are all charged with the job of educating kids.

An Elementary Classroom Teacher's Commentary

The second commentary was written by fourth-grade teacher Virginia Upchurch. She has taught for 25 years, 11 of which have been at Firestone Elementary School. Virginia is a grade-level team leader and has been actively involved in both RITE and TFR since their inception. She was also active in her school's mentoring program and has been the site-based teacher educator for seven student teachers.

Teachers are a unique group of individuals. Most are caring, sharing people. That is why most get into the profession of teaching. What a shock when the reality of teaching collides with the idealism of teaching.

Teachers for the most part love children and the subject matter they embark on in teaching. Special-subject teachers love music, physical education, art, or resource subjects. They have a great desire to share their knowledge and love for their subject. Many see their subject as being a true self-esteem builder for many students, especially those that don't excel in subjects tested on standardized tests. Slower children sometimes excel in special subjects more than in the academics. Special-subject teachers see themselves as "enrichers" of children's lives. I have been as guilty as many other teachers of not recognizing the importance of the subject matter taught by the special-subject teachers and not recognizing the love they have for their subject.

These teachers embark on a teaching career, as most teachers do, with big dreams and visions. Most, as this teacher did, seek input from others to improve their teaching. They search out and ask their principals (the instructional leaders) for help. What a shock when this teacher asks for informal input from the principal, only to discover that the principal doesn't have the time or the specialized subject-matter knowledge. The ideal picture of the instructional leader begins to gradually change. The teacher may even become a little jaded when she realizes that the only input she probably will receive will be in the form of a formal evaluation. The teacher is crying out to the instructional leader for ideas to become a better teacher. But in reality, she usually receives comments that tend to be more formal than the informal input that was originally requested. Gradually this teacher,

who clearly loves her subject matter, comes to realize that the evaluation requirement must override her own teaching beliefs about her subject. Occasionally an
assistant principal becomes a friend and mentor for the idea-seeking teacher.

Often the special-subject teachers are isolated from their peers because they
are the only persons in their building teaching their subject. There is no one to
share ideas with. Instead of a professional family atmosphere, as expected by the
teacher in this case, she finds herself isolated, physically and professionally, from
the other staff members. But the teacher is aware that she is doing a good job teaching. This special-subject teacher did find some input and sharing through the
meetings with her peers set up by the district coordinator. Less isolation was felt
because of those experiences.

As the year progressed this special-subject teacher realized that certain management techniques were expected in the building. Even though it was not exactly
her idea of management, she learned to fall in line with the building techniques.
This was required to fit in. After 3 years a management system was worked out,
but with so much lost time.

This same story is played out yearly in so many schools. This teacher and
many others need ways to communicate their needs to regular classroom teachers
in a professional way. Often, experienced teachers believe that everyone, including special-subject teachers, knows what is expected in a building, especially
management techniques. This feeling of isolation can continue due to lack of understanding by the academic teacher of the subject matter being taught by the special-
subject teacher. Teachers can help other teachers by walking in their classroom
shoes more often. This would lead to a better understanding of each other's problems and needs.

Special-subject teachers are often a group of their own in the building. They
can provide moral support but not professional support for each other. They don't
get to share teaching experiences due to the wide range of subjects taught. I hope
to reach out more from now on to special-subject teachers. More information
between special-subject teacher and classroom teacher needs to be shared. They
have information everyone could use. This could benefit everyone. I wish all classroom teachers could read these comments and have a way to help the isolated
special-subject teachers.

I'm happy this teacher has made the "adjustment" to the building but feel it
could have been made much easier and quicker if the academic teachers took the
time and interest to help, to reach out to all new teachers. It's too bad this happens
over and over again. There has to be a solution, such as mentors. As an experienced teacher, it does remind me of the first-year expectations other teachers had
of me. The isolation could be a factor in why some special-subject teachers and
new teachers give up the profession. Some can't reach out as this one eventually
did. They may not be as "strong" an individual as this special-subject teacher, who
did learn to reach out on her own and adapt. What happens to those who can't do

as she did? Do they continue to be isolated or do they give up a profession they love and could really contribute to?

Too often academic classroom teachers just assume special-subject teachers know what is expected. We are amazed and shocked when they don't. I'm sure I have been guilty of isolating someone over my years of teaching. All teachers need to relate and remember "poor" building experiences and help. They need to reach out to other teachers in all subjects.

THE UNIVERSITY TEAM'S REFLECTIONS

All four composites clearly show the need for schools to build in structures for fostering various forms of reflection and for working with other adults. In our earlier discussion of reflection, we gave examples of reflective activities that we saw during our project. We meant to show that reflective activities may occur among different groups of individuals in relation to different structures. This we believe is positive. The novice academic teacher's cluster meetings provided a formal structure wherein teachers met regularly to talk about common concerns. But in the special-subject teacher story, we clearly saw a need for some sort of structure that would permit professional reflective activities with other teachers in the building.

In addition to building structures that provide a time and a place for reflection, schools must also recognize that the social and emotional needs of beginning teachers cannot be ignored. If schools are to include formal structures that encourage professional reflective activities, they must also recognize that these activities, by their very nature, may produce interpersonal conflict. While students' self-esteem has received much publicity of late, there has been little attention to the building of teachers' self-esteem. The ways in which teachers' self-esteem is increased was evident in each of the composites. Receiving notes from principals and other teachers for a job well done and having the opportunity to share one's expertise with other groups of educators are good examples of esteem-raising activities. The composites make several references to social occasions where teachers came together for meals or to accomplish a task. These occasions were valued by all participants, but for novices they are especially important as a way to get acquainted and feel accepted by others in the school. Teachers also feel positive when they feel they are helping the school or helping other teachers. On the negative side, when teachers are criticized by colleagues, they can become so disheartened that they will either leave teaching or change schools. It is easy for teachers to become discouraged when they are working in isolation and do not receive encouragement from peers and administrators.

Just as individual teachers have different learning needs at various times during their careers, they also may need diverse forms of reflective activities at different times. For example, we might expect novice teachers to engage in more technical analysis of their teaching, while 20-year veterans may benefit more from communal interpretations of experience. We hasten to add, however, that these needs may be reversed when, for example, an experienced teacher takes on a new course or changes schools.

As we have noted elsewhere in this book, professional reflective activities include a wide range of actions that take place among a community of educators. These actions may include, but are not limited to, the assumption of leadership roles within the school, collaboration with a university researcher related to classroom or schoolwide issues, and inquiry as a vehicle for professional growth and problem solving (Holland, Clift, & Veal, 1992). And we would assert that these activities should be available to and expected of both experienced and novice teachers. However, the composites show the importance of recognizing individual needs for professional growth. Beginning teachers arrive at their first year with very different backgrounds of preparation for teaching. Therefore, it should not be assumed that all first-year teachers have the same learning needs any more than it can be assumed that all principals are alike. Experienced teachers also have different needs for professional growth, resources, and reflection with other adults. The individual stories on which these composites were based clearly demonstrate the need to attend to the person as well as the role group.

CHAPTER 6

A Last Chapter Only for This Book—The Themes and the Stories Continue

Sometimes, we lose hope. We read about what is wrong with schools, with teachers, students, parents, universities, communities, policies, and practically anything else remotely related to the process of education. We list the crises of insufficient funds, insufficient prestige; we decry overly sufficient public attention to problems without accompanying solutions. We get caught up in the pains and the realities of daily struggles; we focus on being objectified, perhaps even victimized, by persons and institutions over which we have no control and about which we may not even have knowledge. In acknowledging and analyzing the problems we can forget to search for and celebrate the possibilities.

Time for Reflection was not and is not an example of the way all school–university relationships ought to be. It was not and is not an example of improved test scores through action research (or any other kind of research for that matter). It was and is an example of women and men taking a part of their collective futures into their own hands. It was and is a story of the excitement and the progress that can be made with a little time, a little money, and a concentrated, but temporally bounded effort on working toward shared dreams.

Time for Reflection, which began as an outgrowth of a school–university collaboration for initial teacher preparation, evolved into a multifaceted project that incorporated teacher research, collaborative leadership, action science, and professional reflective activity at various times throughout its funded lifespan. As the composite cases and their commentaries suggest, Time for Reflection provided an opportunity for individual, professional growth through the development of a temporary community of educators. It provided school personnel with resources to accomplish some goals for improving the work environment for novice teachers, experienced teachers, and students. It enabled educators to share leadership responsibilities without competing for full power or ultimate authority. And it provided considerable insight into the ways educators from across institutions can work productively, sometimes joyously, with one another. In the preceding chapters we have shared the story of how the project developed, the stories of individual schools, and the composite stories of individuals with whom we interacted. In this last chapter we want to bring you, the reader, into our discussions by identifying what we feel to be important issues, providing our current thoughts on these issues, and then to raise additional questions about the relevance of our work for those who seek to reform education at all levels, pre-K through adult. Today, 4 years after our last network meeting, the experiences we shared have made a lasting impact on the way we, the five co-authors, view professional education, collaboration, and educational research.

PROFESSIONAL EDUCATION

Reforming education at any level is not easy (Cuban, 1990; Fullan, 1991; Sarason, 1991). We encountered four obstacles that were especially difficult in our attempts to share leadership for changing professional education within and across institutions.

1. Limitations imposed by role definition
2. Implicit and explicit conceptions of what it means to work as a professional within a given institution
3. Implicit and explicit conceptions of professional learning
4. Competition among educators for attention and career advancement

In the following sections we discuss the first two obstacles as they relate to one another, and then discuss each of the last two separately.

Institutional Role Definitions of Professional Work

Within Time for Reflection we sought to remove some of the barriers created by rigid role definitions and institutional constructions of professional work. While we all began with a sense of who we were professionally and what our role was within professional education, we quickly found that all participants needed to maintain flexibility with regard to role definition. We also found that by modifying our roles as we interacted across the conceptual and physical miles that separated schools from the university and from one another, we also changed our conceptions of university work, teachers' work, and administrators' work.

The university story tells of professors in three departments working together to team teach within preservice education and to begin, slowly, merging preservice education with continuing professional development for preservice students, novice teachers, experienced teachers, principals, graduate students, and university faculty. In so doing, our academic specializations and our daily tasks moved from fairly rigid expectations to a more ambiguous, improvisational montage of activities. For example, a visit to a school might include a conference with a preservice student about a lesson plan, a discussion of how to help a first-year teacher, an emotionally charged exchange about a recent district decision that affects personnel, and a reflective discussion with a principal about the notion of empowerment as it played out in a recent team meeting. Such a visit might take no more than 4 hours, with the university liaison rapidly switching from one focus to another while, at the same time, remaining cognizant that she would always be labeled as a "university" representative, as opposed to an individual acting on her own.

Likewise, our roles as researchers also became more diffused over the course of the project. As we have already noted, our conceptions of the boundaries between what is defined as research and what is defined as intervention and what is defined as courtesy became considerably blurred. In some instances, boundaries simply did not exist. It was not uncommon for a teacher to talk with a university staff member about difficulties within a particular team—often these were partially interpersonal conflicts. These were recorded in our fieldnotes as data (research as systematic data collection), along with any advice on group dynamics and shared reflections on the difficulty of collaborative work in general (supportive intervention). We also recorded our attempts to reassure the teacher that he or she was not a bad person, that his or her work was valued, and that progress was, indeed, often a product of conflict (courtesy). These records then all became part of our data (back to research), although we must acknowledge that much of our data were strongly affected by the professional and interpersonal relationships formed among *all* participants.

So were the institutional barriers. For many of the participants, relationships, not roles, became a strong force in decisions about project participation. In defining the university participants as family friends, and in our concurrence with that definition, by the end of the project most of us were able to relax with one another and to accept that we all had strengths—and weaknesses. Most important, we respected one another's work, even though we knew that we did not want to trade places with each other.

Role diffusion and blurred responsibilities can also be seen among the school participants. The school stories tell of teachers who sought and accepted responsibilities previously assumed to belong only to the principals in their particular schools. Teachers calling meetings, seemingly a simple action, brought about a major move from waiting for someone else to take charge to actively assuming responsibility for project success in several of the schools. Teachers began influencing school policy by creating and implementing activities across classrooms and across grades. In one case, teachers also began influencing district priorities by collecting and analyzing data and then designing a pilot project that addressed some of the issues they had identified.

Teachers and administrators began to reach consensus on the desirability of sharing some (not all) school leadership decisions. Within our five schools, principals were at first afraid that they would burden teachers by asking them to run meetings, make decisions about policy, and create social as well as academic extracurricular opportunities for students. Over the 3 years, this fear was virtually erased because the teachers generated expectations for themselves and principals supported their activities, their successes, and their failures. For example, the middle school's tutorial for students and their parents was staffed totally by volunteer teachers (many of whom had families) who wanted to help students who were struggling. At times, the student and parent turnout for these tutorials was encouraging, but often only a handful of students showed up. Not only did the teachers keep the program alive, but the principal found corporate sponsorship for the program. She could have killed it—there was a formidable security factor, the custodians had to rearrange their schedules, and there was no dramatic increase in grades or in test scores for students. Instead of focusing on these potential negatives, however, she chose to support the teachers' initiative and relied on their judgment about whether to keep the program or let it go.

At this point we can say that based on our data, on reports coming from some of the Accelerated Schools (Levin, 1987, 1988; McCarthy & Levin, 1992) and the Essential Schools (McGreal, in press; Prestine, 1993), and on reports from corporate America (SCANS, 1991), relaxing traditional and presumably rigid divisions between role groups in schools, and districts, encourages creativity and risk taking. Shared leadership and shared responsibility have the potential to alter hierarchical power relations by locating most of the decisions under the control of those most affected by such decisions. Our experience within Time for Reflection suggests that sharing leadership and responsibility across institutions also encourages risk taking and creativity as power relations and role relations change, although we are quick to acknowledge that such relations within or across institutions are never eliminated.

What we are talking about, essentially, is changing the contexts for professional education. Others have discussed this as well (Darling-Hammond, 1994; Levine, 1992). Some plans have been operationalized as professional development schools or professional practice schools, but Time for Reflection was never intended to serve as a prototype for a new, albeit hybrid, organization. It is, however, an example of how a cross-institutional community for professional education can develop over a short period of time. We are also quick to acknowledge that, like many similar projects (Clandinin, Davies, Hogan, & Kennard, 1993; Cochran-Smith & Lytle, 1993; Oja & Smullyan, 1989), the major impact of Time for Reflection was on individuals, not on institutions. The context of Time for Reflection was characterized by an evolutionary, dynamic, and interactive approach to both action and reflection. All participants were quite successful in terms of creating a challenging and even happy environment for ourselves. We were less successful in creating a lasting relationship that could withstand loss of funding and changes in personnel. As we think back on this we wonder if, in part, this is related to the last two barriers we identified, conceptions of professional learning and competition for attention and career advancement.

Professional Learning

Early in our work together, many of the school-based participants looked to us for some indication of the project's goals and the school-based activities they would be expected to undertake. We were not at all sure, but we hoped that something positive would happen from talking about hopes and planning for small changes. This did not fit with some people's expectations of what university folks were supposed to provide for school folks. In one of our conversations with a principal we were compared to a very successful consultant from a neighboring university. The principal noted that the consultant always presented information that gave people something to think about. We, on the other hand, did not give information. The principal was, in fact, not sure that we had done much of anything for her staff.

Two years later, we talked with her about that conversation and told her that it had been a major factor in causing us to stop and re-examine our own beliefs about school and university relationships. While she said she did not remember the interaction, she did note that we had become more actively involved with her team the following year. She then acknowledged that in the 3 years we spent together, everyone had changed. One of the changes she experienced was published in a state journal under the title, "Dictatorship vs. Discipleship" (Lazarine, 1989). Participation and critical, reflective interaction had influenced our conception of how to facilitate learning. At the same time, working together had influenced her conception of working with teachers. Professional learning had become an interactive process with different individuals experiencing different outcomes from a core set of experiences.

At the end of funding, after the last network meeting, the co-authors felt that participation had made a short-term difference in teachers' work lives, but we were not at all sure about what, if any, lasting impact the project had on participants. In December 1993 Renee received a long-distance telephone call from a teacher at Fair who had served on the leadership team. He had been thinking, he said, about some new curriculum innovations in his field of science. As department chair he was now in a position to engage others in conversations about the innovations and he wanted to share some of his plans for feedback. He had already secured his principal's permission to use staff development money to pay substitutes to cover classes so that he could get people to begin talking with one another—to share their own beliefs about science teaching. He went on to cite the importance of Time for Reflection in changing his thinking about how people might or might not accommodate new forms of instruction.

Not only is professional learning interactive, with core experiences having different impacts on different individuals, but individuals call on those experiences differentially when necessary. That is, experiences and reflections on those experiences may be stored until they are needed, and then reshaped and reconfigured to fit current circumstances. As the next example illustrates, emotional as well as cognitive factors intertwine in professional learning.

One of the participants returned her commentary on a composite case with a note providing us with an update of all that was still continuing in her school after funding had ended. Some former members had left the team and school, but new members had been added and many of the projects were still operating. She pointed out that it had not taken them long to realize that the continued success of the project had much more to do with what they did to support one another than with what the network did, but still she missed the network. One year later, in a conversation with Marlene, she recalled tears coming to her eyes whenever she received chapter drafts. Clearly, professional learning cannot be reduced to a formula, nor can it be thought of in simple terms such as skill acquisition or knowledge growth. Interaction, time, cognition, and emotion are all intertwined in the constructive learning process.

Competition and Career Advancement

The last barrier we learned about is that of competition among individuals for ownership of ideas and for career advancement. We should note that four of the five co-authors are no longer working at the University of Houston. Renee, Mary Lou, Marlene, and Jane all left for what they perceived to be better opportunities to pursue their careers. Renee, Mary Lou, and Jane are still very much involved with school and university partnerships. Marlene works with school improvement teams, but through the auspices of a regional service center, not a university. Pat, who is still on faculty at the University of Houston, is no longer engaged with the five schools from Time for Reflection, although she continues to work for change in the education of school administrators in several collaborative projects.

As of 1993–94, two of the schools have new principals, and many of the teachers with whom we worked have moved to other schools. Only one of the schools, Woods, still has strong collaborative ties to the university. The others still accept student teachers, but the preservice program called RITE has radically changed from the concept implemented by Renee and Jane. It is no longer a cross-departmental collaboration, although courses are still taught in more than one department. Use of technology and innovative instruction are the ideas that are catching the excitement of the current University of Houston teacher educators. Reflection as a topic that occupies professors' writing and speaking has become passé, although collaboration for teacher education has not.

In other words, as faculty, teachers, and administrators receive opportunities to advance, they leave institutions, which recruit new faculty, teachers, and administrators who have new ideas. These new recruits are often unaware of what has transpired before their arrival. In addition, they often do not wish to be trapped by the ideas of their predecessors. Although individual educators may carry their learning with them, educational organizations import new individuals, and there is little, if any, organizational memory or continuity, *unless* those who remain in the institution make sure that the organizational memory stays alive. Broadstreet Middle School is one such example of teachers working to keep what was learned, and to improve upon it year by year. Suburban School District is an example of how a district can keep a project alive, even though teachers transfer to new schools or to administrative positions.

A final example comes, not from our project, but from Marlene's dissertation (Johnson, 1993b). For 2 years she studied a school near Houston with a reputation for excellence in governance and instruction. Hollibrook Elementary in Spring Branch Independent School District (its real name) was affiliated with Accelerated Schools, a project directed by Henry (Hank) Levin from Stanford University. During the first year of Marlene's work, a new principal arrived with his own ideas, his own vision of Hollibrook's future, and his own team of assistants. She captured the problems, the tensions, and the triumphs as the teachers and the administrators learned to work with one another. Although the learning and the negotiating continued into the second year of her study, it was clear that the "idea" that defined Hollibrook had survived a change in administration, but only because the school participants made a commitment and acted for such survival. Shared leadership for school change had become a plausible reality as opposed to a struggle for power between educators labeled administrators and those labeled teachers.

Eliminating the traditional boundaries between designated leaders and followers in schools does not imply some great anarchy. Quite the contrary. Leadership, as it was best exercised in the Time for Reflection project, was shared among individuals, and done so on the basis of the knowledge, interests, and experience of those assuming a leadership role at any given point in time. Over the course of the project a common understanding emerged about the constraints imposed when leadership is rigidly ascribed only to certain individuals and groups. Not only is there often no way for followers' ideas to be considered, but there is also a hesitancy to change any aspect of a school's functioning for fear of overstepping one's role as either leader or follower. Even more limiting is the lack of a spirit of experimentation where ideas and actions can be tried and studied to determine their relative effectiveness, and where no one—leader or follower—has to always get it right the first time. Shared leadership opens the possibility for ideas and direction to emerge from any point within a school community, and for commitment to those ideas and directions to be a communal decision, rather than an administrative directive.

We feel strongly that both researchers and practitioners need to pay careful attention to the contexts that sustain commitments to collaboration and shared leadership. While individual professional learning and education are important, we feel that a good deal of time, energy, and money is lost when people carry their learning with them and institutions are not able to accumulate long-term benefits. While competition for success is part of the U.S. school and corporate culture, perhaps the sharing, critiquing, and transforming of ideas through collaboration for success may have a stronger, more positive impact on the adults and the children who work in these cultures.

COLLABORATION

In wartime, the term *collaboration* often has been synonymous with treason. Perhaps some of us carry this definition in our heads as we protect our patents, lesson plans, perfectly written paragraphs, and other secrets from those who would steal them for their own profit (whether financial or professional). Our experiences in Time for Reflection partially lead us to that conclusion, but the evidence we collected suggests—even more strongly—that the way we structure our professional work lives makes collaboration very difficult. The following two examples illustrate the difficulty in first creating and then maintaining a work environment that encourages collaboration.

The Woods faculty were among the most enthusiastic respondents to our invitation to figure out what Time for Reflection would become. In the first meeting, when seven schools were considering participation, the principal and the faculty astonished everyone with accounts of the many events that brought the Woods faculty together, such as trips during spring break and other local social events. This school was also one of the strongest proponents of continuing the project, even when three other schools from Urban School District withdrew. But for Woods, getting the project off the ground proceeded very slowly. In part, the slowness was because of unanticipated numbers at the beginning of the school year. In the main, however, the principal and the faculty did not know how to work through a district mandate limiting faculty meetings and professional staff gatherings. Using professional workdays and after-school time to meet was, for several months, prohibited. What had been intended as a protection for teachers became an inhibitor of collaboration and collaborative professional planning.

In contrast, one year later, the Fair team (also in Urban School District) learned from the other schools about the value of using project money to buy time so that teachers might work and plan together. Their principal, at the time, had given the team carte blanche to proceed in whatever way they wished. Plans, actions, and evaluations all proceeded at a rapid pace as the Fair team quickly caught up with their four counterparts. At the final network meeting, the principal vowed to keep the work going even though project money would no longer be available. But he was transferred. In the fall, after the project was officially over, the university team shared the second profile with an uninterested audience comprising the former leadership team—who were then charged with renovating the teachers' lounge as a result of an administrative directive. They felt that all of their progress toward teacher-led decision making had been punished.

If there is only one lesson to be learned from Time for Reflection and other, similar projects around the world it is that collaboration is not easy. Nor is it currently a process embedded within the cultures of most educational enterprises. Our experiences, and our data, lead us to conclude that those who wish to develop and sustain collaboration are well advised to attend to the ambiguity inherent in collaborative relationships, the time-intensive and emotionally intensive commitment, and the importance of occasions for coming together as well as for drawing apart. To illustrate these we draw from the school–university interactions and from interactions among the teams, including our own.

Learning to Embrace Ambiguity

We have mentioned the early ambiguity as university and school participants began trying to work productively across institutions. While we were successful in resolving this for ourselves and with the schools, ambiguity was a characteristic throughout the project as roles were modified and as information was shared. We can identify at least four types of occasions in which ambiguity was most intense.

1. Any time a new person or group of people joined a team or the project
2. Any time data were shared with a group or a team
3. Any time there was disagreement about goals, directions, or commitment
4. Any time the project was (is) discussed publicly

Each of the teams, including the university team, gained and lost participants throughout the life of the project. Whenever this occurred, the original members needed to stop and share information with the newcomer. At the same time, the newcomer asked questions and offered observations, thus prompting the original members to explain, and sometimes to defend, their actions. One example of this was when the Broadstreet team moved into their second year. New people joined the group while, at the same time, new committees were beginning to be formed within the school. The new member questions, "What does this team do?" and "Should I join this team?" were asked along with the remaining member questions, "Are we really making a contribution to the school?" and "Do we need to continue as a committee?" After these questions were discussed privately among individuals, they were aired and resolved publicly in a meeting the university team was asked to facilitate. After that meeting no one was exactly sure what had been accomplished, but at least we all knew that we valued working with one another. Resolution came over the next few months as Broadstreet team members began to make concrete plans and set them in motion.

A second example was when Fair joined the project one year after the other schools. Their entry prompted the university team to wonder how we would manage to spread project personnel and financial resources to a fifth school, when we felt hard pressed to work with the original four. Some university team members stated that they would not work with the new school at all—they simply had no more to give. Some team members then questioned the meaning of collaboration within the university team if we were to establish rigid lines of work responsibility. Still other team members felt that the existence of an argument at all was uncomfortable and problematic. As with the Broadstreet team, these concerns were aired publicly and privately, but not resolved in a single meeting. Over time, they were resolved, but it is impossible to identify when resolution occurred.

It is somewhat easier to identify when ambiguity surrounding the sharing of data and analysis was resolved because of the nature of the school profiles and the feedback from schools about the profiles. Early in the project, before the university team had formulated the concept of a school profile, there was considerable ambiguity concerning what data were to be shared with whom, by whom, and in what form. This was a hotly debated issue in the team, and one that continued for a year. This debate was not confined to the team, for as we reported earlier, school participants wanted to know what we "knew" about their schools and their projects. Resolution occurred over a summer when the university team members openly debated forms and procedures for sharing information. Once tentative agreement was reached, the plans for sharing were cleared with the teams.

After each school team responded, and after the first profile-sharing session, the school teams gave critical feedback on the process. This enabled the university team to feel that the issue of sharing was, at least temporarily, resolved. The second profile-sharing session would be, we thought, fairly straightforward. The ambiguity related to the second profile-sharing session occurred after the second profiles were presented, because many of the team members were absent from the sessions and because the school team members really did not want to use the time to think through our profiles—they wanted to share what they had been through since the project ended. They wanted to talk openly, with people who cared, about their current school experiences. We wanted to verify our interpretations. This leads to a third occasion for ambiguity—those times when goals, directions, and commitments were not shared.

The best example of this ambiguity (which has not yet been entirely resolved) is this book. We have mentioned fairly often that writing for publication was valued by the university participants, but not all five of us shared the same drive to write and rewrite chapter after chapter of the book. And, the commitment to writing for publication was even more varied among our school colleagues. Some of them were excited about participating, while others were suspicious of the university team's motives. Some were eager to write, while others were eager to respond, while still others probably do not know that a book has been produced at all. In other words, collaborative writing and joint publication are not areas in which there are rules to follow—there is no APA or MLA manual for collaborative authorship.

Another example of intense ambiguity surrounding divergence in commitment, direction, and goals occurred when a group member did not want to commit time or energy to any given project. Not only did other members wonder if their recalcitrant colleague was still involved with the project; they also wondered if their own commitment might, indeed, be questionable.

These feelings were exacerbated if the dissenter was a designated team leader or a school administrator. In arguing for a particular project, members ran the risk of confrontation at best, or reprisal at worst. Sometimes, either in writing or in disagreeing, ambiguity was not resolved, and individuals opted to withdraw from the collaboration temporarily or, in some cases, permanently. This, therefore, raises the level of ambiguity in the fourth area, the public sharing of project events.

We have tried to admit that in writing this book we present a university perspective, but have attempted to share the schools' perspective and voices whenever possible. By now it should be clear that there is no such construct as the "university perspective." There is the negotiated report, but if you were to interview each of us separately you would find that each of us would not tell the same story of project involvement. There is, however, the perspective of those who took major responsibility for writing as approved or modified by those who took major responsibility for responding.

This was true for all participants throughout Time for Reflection. When the Pine Grove team members shared their project at a state convention, they emphasized the events in their school and downplayed the network affiliations with the university or the other schools. When the principals from the schools shared their thoughts on the project at a national convention, they emphasized the administrative perspective, not the classroom perspective, and so on. When sharing an event or a story with others, it is virtually impossible to represent all of the participants all of the time; a perfect synthesis does not exist. Some ambiguity can be reduced because of the data we collected throughout, our attempts at triangulation, and our attempts to identify disconfirming evidence and discrepant examples, but it can never be eliminated. Any report of a collaboration is just one report—never *the* report.

At the same time, sharing the story with others can, itself, promote an occasion to reflect on project meaning, scope, and process. Public sharing can force participants to examine their diverse perspectives and to identify areas of agreement as well as areas of disagreement that can, themselves, be discussed with others. We did not find that disagreement was a barrier to collaboration, but we did find that learning to deal with disagreements (with being personally disagreeable) was essential. Collaboration does not just happen—it requires considerable effort to begin and even more effort to maintain.

Committing Time and Emotional Energy

At the end of 3 years we could optimistically say that we were finally beginning to learn how to work productively with one another and with our public school colleagues. We apologetically note, however, that 3 years is not a sufficient amount of time in which to produce systemic collaboration. We have come to realize that moving from an essentially individualistic culture to a more collaborative culture is a dynamic process that itself includes the dimensions that we referred to in Chapter 2 in our discussions of a professional learning culture. Three of those dimensions are especially relevant here—leadership, individual, and interpersonal.

Leadership for collaboration means that some people must begin the process. In our case those individuals included

1. The university-based and field-based educators who agreed to work together to establish RITE, the University of Houston teacher education innovation that enabled educators to meet across institutions
2. The subset of the RITE faculty who sought external funding to move program development beyond initial teacher preparation, toward continued learning for all educators
3. The school district and College of Education administrators who supported the extension through moderate resource allocation and verbal signals that such an extension was desirable
4. The teachers and principals who volunteered to think through the possibilities
5. The Danforth Foundation administrators who encouraged the proposal through advice and, eventually, funding

The "beginning" took over a year. The beginning required time for writing, formal and informal meetings, telephone conversations, and numerous visits to the university campus, the schools, the district offices, and even homes so that planning to begin might occur. The beginning required positive emotional energy to reassure the participants that participation was both voluntary and valued. The assistant professors needed to feel comfortable that involvement would not cost them their jobs. The teachers, principals, graduate students, and professors needed to feel that risks were valued by school and college administrators. The university and school administrators needed to feel that the project would not harm K–12 or university students. We could go on with this list, but by now it should be evident that beginnings need an emotional climate that calms fears. Throughout the project calming was necessary from principals who also served as evaluators and from administrators who continued to provide moderate resources and verbal encouragement.

Another aspect of the emotional climate includes an element of excitement, or the feeling that the project is both valuable and enjoyable. While leadership is certainly a factor in promoting excitement, we found that beginning Time for Reflection was helped by key individuals on the university campus and in the schools, whose excitement was contagious. A memorable example of this was the Broadstreet team, who came to early meetings with their ideas about what they could do in their school. While team members from other schools struggled to define their relationship to the project, the Broadstreet teachers were literally bouncing up and down with excitement as they planned their various subprojects.

Individuals helped maintain the excitement throughout the project. On the university team, Diane Durbin was one of the original graduate students in the first year of the project. Because of her commitment to her job as a school librarian, she could not work with us full time, or even part time. She could, however, attend some university team meetings and take notes. She was our "guest," and her stories and her questions often lifted our spirits when the ambiguity or the time commitment overwhelmed one or more of the university team members.

The school stories, and especially the composite cases, included numerous examples of interpersonal tension and interpersonal encouragement. We have learned that the interpersonal dynamics among collaborators cannot be ignored. Indeed, they must be attended to very carefully. Sometimes this meant a phone call or a visit to say, "Are you OK?" Sometimes it meant an apology (either overt or implied) for giving offense. Most often, however, it meant verbal and nonverbal reassurance that people enjoyed and even valued one another within the teams and across the teams. When faculty from one school visited the campus of another school, our fieldnotes recorded accounts of joy and enthusiasm by the hosts. When the university team arranged for food at network meetings, our fieldnotes recorded appreciation for the symbolic as well as the overt action on our part. In contrast, when people left a team or when progress was dramatically halted, it was often because participants did not feel that they were a valued part of the effort. Other times people left because they had so many other commitments that they felt as though continued participation would only let the other team members down, which leads us to the final lesson we learned about collaboration.

Establishing Rituals for Coming Together and Drawing Apart

In some writing (which we will not cite here) authors refer to "true" collaboration or "real" collaboration. Our research and our experiences lead us to conclude that there is no such thing. While we agree with Hord (1986) that sometimes one can distinguish between cooperation and collaboration, we feel that within complex, multifaceted collaborative endeavors such as cross-institutional programs in professional education, there are always elements of both. Cooperation, we believe, is an agreement in which goals are not necessarily shared between the cooperating individuals or institutions, but the goals are not contradictory. Sharing space, time, or other resources makes sense in that separate goals can be accomplished without much inconvenience and, in most cases, with considerable benefits to all parties. An example of cooperation can be found in certification programs for teacher education and administrator education in which a novice serves as an intern to a more experienced professional. The certifying institution benefits, the novice benefits, and the experienced professional benefits, as they each pursue their separate goals of implementing university-based certification programs, obtaining certification, and facilitating teaching or administering in schools.

Individual goals and benefits are not abandoned in a collaborative project. The key distinction, however, is that the individual goals are subsets of the mutually agreed-upon project goals. An example of this can be found, in embryonic form, in some professional practice schools or professional development schools (Darling-Hammond, 1994; Levine, 1992). In these new institutional arrangements, professional learning is held as a common mission or goal for everyone. This is not to imply that project goals are static. They, like almost everything else, can be renegotiated within the life of the collaboration.

Other examples can be found in school reform efforts such as the Accelerated School Project (Levin, 1987, 1988) in which cadres of teachers and administrators work together to improve learning opportunities and learning outcomes for students. In coming together to work for a common goal, no one leaves her or his personality, biography, or individuality out of the total picture. Rather, the individuals draw from their strengths (and weaknesses) to negotiate progress. This collection of contributed strengths can enable a global progress toward goals— but progress is not automatic, just as individual participation is not assured.

A key point here is that while collaboration can be nurtured, it cannot be mandated. As Hargreaves and Dawe (1988) point out, there are numerous occasions in schools when people are told they must work together. Such contrived collegiality (their term) is not an example of people agreeing to work together for a common goal. It is an example of a policy carrying the assumption that educators can be made to work in prescribed arrangements.

In our work, both with the schools and with one another, we found that such prescriptions were seldom effective. Teachers and administrators who did not wish to work together simply did not work together. They avoided meetings or sat silent. In some cases they actively worked to sabotage groups through verbal and nonverbal expressions of disapproval. In other words, people who are unhappy about being together can construct a negative professional and interpersonal environment, one that is far more harmful than helpful.

To minimize this possibility and to develop a collaborative culture for professional learning, we feel that three conditions are essential. The first condition is that opportunities to join the collaborative effort remain open to educators throughout the life of the project. The second is that there must be opportunities for participants to withdraw gracefully and legitimately—whether permanently or for a brief period of time. The final is that within the culture there must be opportunities for renewing commitment and reinvigorating those who choose to participate.

An open invitation minimizes (but does not eliminate) the probability that participants will be considered to be an exclusive, elite "club" of learners. The Broadstreet, Firestone, and Fair teams all experienced tension within their schools because they belonged, while others did not. The Broadstreet team worked through this by actively reaching out to new members at the beginning of the school year and again at two or more points throughout the year. The Firestone team worked through the tension by deciding to disband and join new working groups in the school wherein teachers had chosen to work together. At Fair, the problem was not resolved by the team members because the new administration made the decision for all faculty to meet in teams and pursue administratively assigned projects.

Within all of the teams, especially the university team, there were times when members experienced a desire to quit. Personal problems, time demands, conflicting expectations, changes in work responsibilities, and, in some instances, life threatening illnesses made it difficult or impossible to participate in team projects. And yet, members still worked in the same building and interacted with one another in professional settings. It was simply not possible to expect every member to give the project his or her major effort all of the time. To maintain the project and the collaboration, the other members devised implicit and explicit strategies for giving a member "time out" without ostracizing the member from the group. We have already mentioned an example of this in our reference to Diane Durbin's need to withdraw and yet remain a welcome visitor whenever possible.

Our final point is that in defining collaboration as an agreement to work together toward a common goal, it is too easy to take both an individual's agreement and the presumed common goal for granted over time. Assuming individual commitment and agreement can lead one member to make decisions for another, which can engender or exacerbate tension within the group. Our network meetings served as occasions for agreements to be revisited, for commitment to projects to be questioned, examined, and then renewed or abandoned, and for individuals to publicly demonstrate their commitments to one another. Within the university team, the data analysis, profile writing, and debates during the summer and throughout the project served as occasions for renewing our own commitments to reflective practice in general and to Time for Reflection in particular. Through such meetings we were able to clarify some of our thinking and to construct our own understanding of what, for us, was a new form of educational research.

EDUCATIONAL RESEARCH

Our understandings of both reflective practice and educational inquiry at the outset of the project have been transformed. When Time for Reflection began, we held an implicit notion of teachers utilizing resources, creating opportunities, and developing contexts that would enable them to reflect on their teaching practice, thus becoming more skilled and knowledgeable practitioners. We thought, for a time, that this conception was a logical and reasonable extension of what we had begun in RITE, our preservice teacher education program. While we continued to hold this interest throughout the project, over time it became background rather than foreground, for what emerged in each of the school action plans was a much larger role for teachers as they began to assume schoolwide leadership roles. While our original notion of reflective practice certainly included more than just a view of reflection as a technical process limited to evaluating the relative effectiveness of particular teaching activities, we were still thinking about reflective practice as limited to the act of teaching and therefore as something that was concerned with what went on in classrooms.

What we came to understand about reflective practice as it operates in wider school contexts is that discussions of shared goals and collaborative action provide educators with an opportunity to move their thinking to new levels. Not only do they begin to consider their goals and actions in terms of the school as a whole, but they also begin to ask the kinds of questions that can lead to substantive change. Our thinking didn't change all at once or even in one dramatic move. The change was so gradual that it was really only in what Schön would call our "reflection-on-action" that we came to recognize a shift in our thinking about the nature of reflective practice. What was important about that shift was that it expanded the focus of reflective practice beyond individual classrooms to the school itself. This larger arena for reflective practice meant that teachers were now thinking and making decisions about issue and practices that had previously been the exclusive purview of administrators. In other words, school leadership was shared among participants as opposed to being explicitly or even tacitly located in the principal's office.

At the same time, as we discussed in Chapters 1 and 2, we began to revise our understandings of educational inquiry as it operates in a school–university collaborative project. We have described how we came to employ an action science framework to help the leadership teams gather and use information about the effects of their activities. As the university team provided the school teams with information about the consistency of their actions with their espoused theories in action, the leadership teams could confront and resolve conflicts within the school and between the school participants and the university participants. The school teams, in many cases, were able to modify the university participants' research and, at the same time, engage in research themselves. In other words, leadership for the inquiry aspects of the project was being increasingly shared across institutions.

And so we find that it is time to abandon the metaphor we have used throughout this book. Productive educational inquiry within collaborative projects is not conducted by parlor guests, interior designers, or even close family friends because in all three cases the inhabitants are being studied, but the visitors come and go without having to undergo similar scrutiny. Within a collaboration such as ours, all participants were observed and analyzed by the research team. And all participants gave and received feedback from one another, whether they designated themselves as researchers or not. Within Time for Reflection we found that the team that spent the most hours analyzing their actions and working on transforming their practice was (you probably figured this out a long time ago) the university team.

In collaborative projects, wherein reflective practice is a goal, inquiry into inquiry is an important form of reflective practice. What we have learned from our project, and from reading about several other groups who are exploring research within collaborative projects (Clandinin, Davies, Hogan, & Kennard, 1993; Cochran-Smith & Lytle, 1993; Hunsaker & Johnston, 1992), is that the norms and guidelines for this kind of research are not well understood and are certainly not well established, but that it is fundamentally different from what many of us learned to do in our graduate training. It is also far removed from the traditional preparation programs for teachers and administrators.

While teacher preparation and administrator preparation may include information on test construction, experiences working with data on student achievement and attitudes, and introductions to the evaluation of teacher behavior, or even school finance, the application of these skills is seldom, if ever, exercised to systematically study the holistic organization and interrelated functions of the school. In addition, schools have typically formed operating norms that emphasize the appearance of success, not the documentation of problems. Problems, for practitioners, are frequently seen as signs that someone or some group has erred or failed, as opposed to naturally occurring events in any social structure. School problems for academics are viewed in the opposite manner and often are occasions for researchers to go to work.

As teachers, administrators, and researchers begin to create a collaborative, cross-institutional culture, it is important to recognize—and celebrate—the differences all participants contribute. It is also important to acknowledge that different participants have different needs and desires. When the collaboration is beginning, and throughout implementation, it is important that no one group of participants summarily impose the norms of its background cultures on the others. This means an early and continual commitment to negotiating the inquiry as well as the actions. We would like to emphasize that such negotiations are ongoing and are as dynamic as the collaboration itself. Just because an issue is resolved at one time does not mean that it will never reappear again. From our project we have identified five areas of negotiation, which we offer with the intention that others will be added over time.

1. A common language across institutional cultures so that thoughts, ideas, and concerns can be communicated without harming the interinstitutional relationship
2. A recognition of the power and status dynamics inherent within individual institutions, cross-institutional structures, and collaborative inquiry projects
3. An understanding of what questions are important to whom
4. An understanding of who will perform what tasks within the larger inquiry
5. An understanding of what information can be reported to whom in what form

In the following discussion of these five areas, we would like to emphasize that at no time can one assume that all participants share the same, exact understanding at any one time. Checking and rechecking, negotiating and renegotiating are all a part of the ongoing collaborative process.

Common Language

It became obvious to us that the creation of a common language and understanding that crosses institutional cultures does not automatically occur despite a history of working professional relationships. And, even though we were all educators, we belonged to different discourse communities (Gee, 1990) and held different values regarding the way we conducted our work and spent our professional time. For example, the word "problem" was often defined, implicitly, by the university participants as an interesting area for research. But the connotation of "problem," whether openly stated or merely understood, is a divisive concept. For researchers the word represents something to be studied and analyzed, perhaps to be described and better understood, and possibly to be remedied. But often when we said "problem" or even "improvement," teachers and administrators assumed we meant that their schools and their practice were seriously at fault and that we were casting aspersions on their work.

Another example is the use of the word "support." To those of us who worked in the university, support meant facilitating time to plan and time to reflect on one's practice. To many of the school participants, support meant providing ideas, making concrete suggestions for change, and working with teachers in real classrooms. Over time we all learned about the multiple meanings we each brought to seemingly simple terms. Over time we all learned to check for understandings. We also learned to predict and attempt to avoid misunderstandings—much of the time.

Power and Status

School district superintendents have authority over principals; principals have authority over teachers. Even though some school restructuring efforts are at least talking about rearranging some of these relationships, no one involved in public education is talking seriously about eliminating the concept of district. Although one can find remnants of the impact of our project on individuals and on a few school practices, the only action plan that still remains in place today is the first-year teacher mentor program begun by the teachers at Pine Grove. Why? Because they had complete backing from the district office and because their project filled a requirement from the state. We have learned that while any collaborative effort must have ground-level participation and commitment from teachers and administrators, there must also be top-down approval and recognition from all levels of the hierarchy. For educational research to fit into this picture, it must serve the needs of the school and the district as well as the needs of the researchers.

We realize that some research projects and some research questions cannot be asked or answered collaboratively. We also recognize that some teacher research can and should be conducted without participation from the university community. Those points have been elaborated elsewhere, and we do not wish to debate them. We are more concerned with research that occurs within collaborative, inter-institutional relationships. As with everything else within the collaborative, however, the research aspect must be open to negotiation and must ultimately serve the goals of the project without harming either individuals or the institutions involved.

Research Questions

When we began Time for Reflection, we had no specific research questions, but we did have a desire to document the process. The school participants had no research agenda, but they did have questions that could be answered through data collection and analysis. While their questions did not drive our research, we were able to collect data they found useful. For example, as they became interested in developing projects to benefit students and teachers, we became interested in the ways they evaluated the degrees of success or failure within those projects, which led us to assist them with formal evaluations—if they requested us to do so. As we became more interested in the evolution of role relationships throughout the project, we were able to provide them with information on novice teacher/experienced teacher relationships within the project.

In some cases the project did include practitioner-led inquiry. Teachers from Pine Grove, Firestone, Fair, and Broadstreet all designed some form of data collection mechanism to document their work and used that information to make changes in the project. But it would be inaccurate to say that action research or program evaluation became an integral part of the school culture. It would be accurate to say that all of us learned a great deal about the value of looking inward to our own values and assumptions without carelessly arguing that teachers should become more like researchers, or vice versa.

Task Negotiation

Inquiry within a collaborative does not mean that everyone must perform every task, nor does it mean that every participant must be a part of an inquiry team. Some of us like asking questions and designing strategies for answering them. Others enjoy observing, interviewing, and other tasks related to data collection. Some of us like sorting through all of the data to figure out what it means. Others prefer to read and debate the interim and final reports. And so we learned to build task negotiation into the process. This held for inquiries jointly conducted by the university and the school, but it also held within the teams.

The university team was no exception. Although we were all trained in some research techniques, two of the university professors preferred to think conceptually, while two preferred a rich array of data to spur their thinking. Two of the team members were able to combine their data collection with other tasks, while for three members data collection was accomplished on top of a full university teaching and service load. Three of us currently have jobs that give us time to analyze data and write; two of us have jobs that require our presence in action settings, with little time to analyze or write. We found that if we all expected the same effort at the same time from one another, we spent a great deal of time complaining about what was not getting done as opposed to moving our work forward. Within the collaborative endeavor it is important to recognize that all parties cannot be all things to one another.

Reporting of Information

Our last point is the one that was most serious for us. Although we thought we had read widely about qualitative design, action research, and school–university collaboration, we did not consider carefully the ethical dimensions of reporting out data within a collaborative project. We naively felt that by securing permission, ensuring confidentiality, assigning code names, securing fieldnotes, and following a methodologically defensible qualitative design, we had covered all of the areas necessary for our work. We soon realized our mistake as we found we needed to address questions such as: (1) Should any one individual deliberately screen information for others, when the project involves a group of people working with another group of people? (2) When an individual has developed a confidential relationship with another individual, can the information be reported without others immediately knowing the source? (3) To what extent should one engage in perceptual checks with school members? (4) Is it possible to be sufficiently rigorous without causing other participants to experience discomfort or even professional harm?

We do not mean to imply that negative information should be avoided or suppressed. Indeed, much of our work revolved around developing procedures (such as our profile-sharing sessions) that invited all participants to respond to the information and to openly debate the implications. But our focus on process avoided the ethical question in favor of the procedural recommendation. When a group of researchers (whether university-based or school-based) provides feedback to others, the power dimensions of the relationships between the groups are emphasized. In collaborative endeavors, what right does a university team have to impose its evaluations on a school team, regardless of whether the school team is invited to respond? What right does a school team have to impose its evaluations on a university team, regardless of whether the university team is invited to respond?

The answer, we believe, must be placed within a context of mutual investment in the collaboration and concern for a continuous search to improve education for adults and children. All team members must perceive that all parties are acting in good faith. That is, the researchers must be operating from negotiations in good faith with others, not acting unilaterally and expecting the others to approve. Participants must be very clear about their own agendas and their motives for agreeing to participate in a collaborative project. There also must be agreement by all concerned as to what data will be reported to whom and in what form. For example, principals should not request researchers to report on their observations of teachers—unless the teachers want reports to the principal to become part of ongoing project feedback.

Negotiations should be conducted before data collection begins, and any changes must be reauthorized by participants. It is during the negotiation period that issues of language and cultural differences can be identified and resolved as all parties articulate their initial expectations for the project and work toward setting a mutually agreeable action research agenda.

When a group of people from one institution agrees to participate in collaborative action research with another group from a different institution, the result is a complex set of intersecting relationships that pose ethical problems for all concerned. Each relationship includes dynamic elements that vary over the life and settings of the project. In addition, there are numerous reasons why people choose to participate in such projects and why they remain committed to participation. In many cases, ethical issues arise that cannot be anticipated by the original design of the project, and there will not be routines or guidelines in place for resolving these issues. In our project, resolution often focused on the expedient, although each incident also sparked a discussion about how to handle similar situations in the future. We are not satisfied that we have successfully engaged the ethical issues we faced, because, frankly, we feel that we are novices in this realm. We do feel, however, that once we became aware of ethical concerns, we did not simply avoid them in the hope that they would go away. We hope that our discussion of the issues we faced sparks continued dialogue among researcher and practitioner collaborators who feel that they must act responsibly in addition to contemplating the nature of responsible action.

ENDINGS AND NEW BEGINNINGS

Sometimes funding periods end, people move to different towns or different jobs, and both individuals and institutions seem to resist change. Sometimes the ideals or ideas are never put into practice; sometimes they are, but the practical instantiations do not embody the early ideals. Sometimes we become cynical and dwell on promises unkept or premature endings of promising beginnings. We promised in Chapter 1 that the story of Time for Reflection was neither a fairy tale nor a failure. As we come to the end of this set of reflections on the story, we label our joint struggle to learn to work together as a beginning. The lessons we learned here have carried into our continuing work as researchers, teacher educators, and administrative educators. The school colleagues with whom we continue to correspond report that the lessons they learned have been carried into their ongoing commitments to improve educational work settings for teachers, administrators, and children.

Taking responsibility for a dream of educational change that includes collaboration across institutions means, for us, that change is not something that one group prescribes and another enacts. Rather, change is a result of collaboration among people who see themselves as critical friends and who care passionately about one another's well-being. In such collaborations, interventions are not imposed by reformers, but evolve through supportive, reflective analyses on data-based information relating practices and perceptions to procedures and goals. Such collaborative leadership implies a shared responsibility for moving in a direction that enables students, teachers, administrators, university professors, and researchers to continually improve their abilities to help one another succeed.

References

Argyris, C. (1970). *Intervention theory and method*. Reading, MA: Addison-Wesley.

Argyris, C., Putnam, R., & Smith, D. (1985). *Action science*. San Francisco: Jossey-Bass.

Argyris, C., & Schön, D. (1975). *Theory into practice*. San Francisco: Jossey-Bass.

Argyris, C., & Schön, D. (1978). *Organizational learning: A theory of action perspective*. Reading, MA: Addison-Wesley.

Bakhtin, M. M. (1981). Discourse in the novel. In M. Holquist (Ed.), *The dialogic imagination* (pp. 259–422). Austin: University of Texas Press.

Berman, & McLaughlin, M. (1978). *Federal programs supporting educational change: Vol. VIII. Implementing and sustaining innovations*. Santa Monica, CA: Rand Corporation.

Bird, T., & Little, J. W. (1985). *Instructional leadership in eight secondary schools. Final report*. Boulder, CO: Center for Action Research. (ED 263 694)

Bloom, A. (1987). *The closing of the American mind: How higher education has failed democracy and impoverished the souls of today's students*. New York: Simon & Schuster.

Carter, K., Cushing, K., Sabers, D., Stein, P., & Berliner, D. (1988). Expert–novice differences in perceiving and processing visual classroom information. *Journal of Teacher Education, 39*, 25–31.

Cinamond, J. H., & Zimpher, N. L. (1990). Reflectivity as a function of community. In R. T. Clift, W. R. Houston, & M. Pugach (Eds.), *Encouraging reflective practice in education: An analysis of issues and programs* (pp. 57–72). New York: Teachers College Press.

Clandinin, D. J. (1985). Personal practical knowledge: A study of teachers' classroom images. *Curriculum Inquiry, 15*, 361–384.

Clandinin, D. J., Davies, A., Hogan, P., & Kennard, B. (1993). *Learning to teach: Teaching to learn*. New York: Teachers College Press.

Clift, R., Holland, P., & Veal, M. L. (1990). School context dimensions that affect staff development. *Journal of Staff Development, 11*, 34–38.

Clift, R., Houston, W. R., & Pugach, M. (Eds.). (1990). *Encouraging reflective practice in education: An analysis of issues and programs*. New York: Teachers College Press.

Clift, R., Johnson, M., Holland, P., & Veal, M. L. (1992). Developing the potential for collaborative school leadership. *American Educational Research Journal, 28*, 877–908.

Clift, R. T., & Say, M. (1988). Public schools and preservice teacher education: Collaboration or conflict? *Journal of Teacher Education, 39*, 2–7.

Clift, R., Veal, M. L., Johnson, M., & Holland, P. (1990). Restructuring teacher education through collaborative action research. *Journal of Teacher Education, 41*, 52–62.

Cochran-Smith, M., & Lytle, S. (1993). *Inside/outside: Teacher research and knowledge.*
New York: Teachers College Press.

Connelly, F. M., & Clandinin, D. J. (1988). *Teachers as curriculum planners: Narratives
of experience.* New York: Teachers College Press.

Corey, S. (1953). *Action research to improve school practice.* New York: Bureau of Publications, Teachers College, Columbia University.

Cuban, L. (1990). Reforming again, again, and again. *Educational Researcher, 19*, 3–13.

Cunningham, W. G., & Gresso, D. (1993). *Cultural leadership: The culture of excellence
in education.* Boston: Allyn & Bacon.

Darling-Hammond, L. (Ed.). (1994). *Professional development schools: Schools for developing a profession.* New York: Teachers College Press.

Dewey, J. (1933). *How we think.* Boston: Heath.

Edmonds, R. R. (1979). Effective schools for the urban poor. *Educational Leadership,
37*, 15–23.

Elbaz, F. (1983). *Teacher thinking: A study of practical knowledge.* London: Croom Helm.

Elliott, J. (1990). Teachers as researchers: Implications for supervision and for teacher
education. *Teaching and Teacher Education, 6*(1), 1–26.

Elliott, J., & Adelman, C. (1976). *Classroom action research.* Norwich, England: University of East Anglia, Centre for Applied Research in Education.

Fosnot, C. T. (1989). *Enquiring teachers, enquiring learners: A constructivist approach
for teaching.* New York: Teachers College Press.

Fullan, M. (1991). *The new meaning of educational change.* New York: Teachers College Press.

Gee, J. (1990). *Social linguistics and literacies: Ideology in discourses.* London: Falmer.

Good, T., & Brophy, J. (1986). School effects. In M. C. Wittrock (Ed.), *Handbook of
research on teaching* (3rd ed., pp. 570–602). New York: Macmillan.

Griffin, G., Lieberman, A., & Noto, J. (1983). *Final report on interactive research and
development in schools.* New York: Teachers College, Columbia University.

Grossman, P., & Richert, A. (1988). Unacknowledged knowledge growth: A re-examina-
tion of the effects of teacher education. *Teaching and Teacher Education, 4*(1), 53–62.

Hargreaves, A., & Dawe, R. (1988). Paths of professional development: Contrived collegiality, collaborative culture, and the case of peer coaching. *Teaching and Teacher
Education, 6*, 227–242.

Hart, A. W. (1992, April). *The social and organizational influence of principals: Evaluating principals on organizational criteria.* Paper presented at the annual meeting
of the American Educational Research Association, San Francisco.

Hirsch, E. D. (1987). *Cultural literacy: What every American needs to know.* Boston:
Houghton Mifflin.

Hodgkinson, H. (1957). Action research—A critique. *The Journal of Educational Sociology, 31*(4), 137–153.

Holland, P., Clift, R., & Veal, M. L. (1992). Linking preservice and inservice supervision
through professional inquiry. In C. Glickman (Ed.), *Supervision in transition*
(pp. 169–182). Association for Supervision and Curriculum Development.

Hord, S. M. (1986). A synthesis of research on organizational collaboration. *Educational Leadership, 43,* 22–26.

Hunsaker, L., & Johnston, M. (1992). Teacher under construction: A collaborative case study of teacher change. *American Educational Research Journal, 29,* 350–372.

Johnson, M. (1993a, April). *Defining and negotiating leadership roles: Learning from Hollibrook Elementary School.* Paper presented at the annual meeting of the American Educational Research Association, Atlanta.

Johnson, M. (1993b). A study of shared leadership within an elementary school. Unpublished doctoral dissertation. University of Houston.

Lanzara, G. F. (1991). Shifting stories: Learning from a reflective experiment in a design process. In D. A. Schön (Ed.), *The reflective turn: Case studies in and on educational practice* (pp. 285–320). New York: Teachers College Press.

Lazarine, D. (1989). Dictatorship vs. discipleship: Leadership vs. lendership. *Instructional Leader,* 8–9.

Levin, H. M. (1987). New schools for the disadvantaged. *Teacher Education Quarterly, 14*(4), 60–83.

Levin, H. M. (1988). Accelerating elementary education for disadvantaged students. In Chief State School Officers (Eds.), *School success for students at risk* (pp. 209–225). Orlando, FL: Harcourt Brace Jovanovich.

Levine, M. (Ed.). (1992). *Professional practice schools: Linking teacher education and school reform.* New York: Teachers College Press.

Lewin, K. (1948). Resolving social conflicts. *Selected papers on group dynamics.* New York: Harper & Row.

Lewin, K. (1951). *Field theory in social science.* New York: Harper & Row.

Lieberman, A. (1992). The meaning of scholarly activity and the building of community. *Educational Researcher, 21,* 5–12.

Little, J. W. (1982). Norms of collegiality and experimentation: Workplace conditions of school success. *American Educational Research Journal, 19*(3), 325–340.

Livingston, C., & Castle, S. (Eds.). (1989). *Teachers and research in action.* Washington, DC: National Education Association.

McCarthy, J., & Levin, H. (1992). Accelerated schools for students in at-risk situations. In H. C. Waxman et al. (Eds.), *Students at-risk in at-risk schools.* Newbury Park, CA: Corwin.

McClure, R., & Watts, G. (1990). Expanding the contract to revolutionize school renewal. *Phi Delta Kappan, 71,* 765–774.

McGreal, T. (in press). Creating an essential school: Lessons learned. *Journal of Educational Administration.*

McLaughlin, M. (1993). What matters most in teachers' workplace context? In J. W. Little & M. McLaughlin (Eds.), *Teachers' work: Individuals, colleagues, and contexts* (pp. 79–103). New York: Teachers College Press.

Miles, M. B., & Huberman, A. M. (1984). *Qualitative data analysis.* Beverly Hills, CA: Sage.

Milstein, M. M. (Ed.). (1993). *Changing the way we prepare educational leaders: The Danforth experience.* Thousand Oaks, CA: Corwin.

Noffke, S. (1992). The work and workplace of teachers in action research. *Teaching and Teacher Education, 8,* 15–29.

Oja, S., & Smullyan, L. (1989). *Collaborative action research*. London: Falmer.

Peshkin, A. (1978). *Growing up American*. Chicago: University of Chicago Press.

Peters, T. J., & Waterman, R. H. (1982). *In search of excellence*. New York: Macmillan.

Piaget, J. (1926). *The language and thought of the child*. New York: Harcourt Brace.

Prestine, N. (1993). Feeling the ripples, riding the waves. In J. Murphy & P. Hallinger (Eds.), *Restructuring schooling: Learning from ongoing efforts*. New York: Corwin.

Rosenholtz, S. J. (1989). *Teacher's workplace: The social organization of schools*. New York: Longman.

Rousseau, J. J. (1979). *Emile* or *On education* (A. Bloom, Trans.). New York: Basic Books. (Original work published *circa* 1764)

Rudduck, J. (1985). *Humanities Curriculum Project: An introduction* (rev. ed.). London: Schools Council Publications.

Sarason, S. B. (1991). *The predictable failure of educational reform*. San Francisco: Jossey-Bass.

SCANS. (1991, June). *What work requires of schools: A SCANS report for America 2000*. Washington, DC: U.S. Department of Labor, The Secretary's Commissions on Achieving Necessary Skills.

Schön, D. A. (1971). *Beyond the stable state*. New York: Norton.

Schön, D. A. (1983). *The reflective practitioner: How professionals think in action*. New York: Basic Books.

Sizer, T. (1984). *Horace's compromise: The dilemma of the American high school*. Boston: Houghton Mifflin.

Stenhouse, L. (1983). The relevance of practice to theory. *Theory Into Practice, 22*, 211–215.

Stenhouse, L. (1985). A note on case study and educational practice. In R. G. Burgess (Ed.), *Field methods in the study of education* (pp. 263–271). Philadelphia: Falmer.

Sussman, L. (1979). *Tales out of school: Implementing organizational change in elementary grades*. Philadelphia: Temple University Press.

Tripp, D. (1989, June). Collaborative research: Definitions and an educational agenda. In M. Wodlinger (Ed.), *Collaborative action research in Canadian teacher education*. Proceedings of the Third Invitational Conference of the Canadian Association of Teacher Education, Laval Universitie, Ste-Foy, Quebec.

Van Manen, M. (1977). Linking ways of knowing with ways of being practical. *Curriculum Inquiry, 6*, 205–228.

Veal, M. L., Clift, R., & Holland, P. (1989). School contexts that encourage reflection: Teacher perceptions. *International Journal of Qualitative Studies in Education, 2*, 315–333.

Von Glaserfeld, E. (1989). Cognition, construction of knowledge, and teaching. *Synthese, 80*, 121–140.

Vygotsky, L. S. (1962). *Thought and language*. Cambridge, MA: MIT Press.

Waxman, H. C., deFelix, J. W., Anderson, J. E., & Baptiste, H. P. (1992). *Students at risk in at-risk schools*. Thousand Oaks, CA: Corwin.

Wildman, T. M., & Niles, J. A. (1987). Reflective teachers: Tensions between abstractions and realities. *Journal of Teacher Education, 38*, 25–31.

Zeichner, K. (1981). Reflective teaching and field-based experience in teacher education. *Interchange, 12*, 1–22.

Index

About the Authors

Renee Tipton Clift is an Associate Professor of curriculum and instruction at the University of Illinois at Urbana-Champaign. She received her Ph.D. from Stanford University in 1984, where she majored in curriculum and teacher education, with a minor in psychology. She is co-editor of *Encouraging Reflective Practice in Education: An Examination of Issues and Programs* and *Focal Points: Qualitative Inquiries into Teaching and Teacher Education.* Her journal publications include articles on learning to teach English, school/university collaboration, and forms of school leadership. She is the recipient of the 1992–93 University of Illinois College of Education Scholar Award and the Conference on English Education, Richard A. Meade Award for Distinguished Research in English Education, in 1988 and again in 1993. Her current research focuses on the promise of electronic communication for enhancing teacher learning and school/university collaboration.

Mary Lou Veal is an Assistant Professor at the University of North Carolina at Greensboro in the department of exercise and sport science. She received her Ed.D. in 1986 from Teachers College, Columbia University in curriculum and instruction in physical education. Prior to her doctoral work, Mary Lou taught physical education for 16 years in Denton and Dallas, Texas and served as a cooperating teacher for more than 30 student teachers. In addition to her work in *Time for Reflection,* she has investigated physical education teachers' assessment practices and the meaning they give to pupil assessment. Her current work is focused on the effects of incorporating authentic and performance assessment into the instructional process in physical education. She is a Fellow of the Research Consortium, American Alliance of Health, Physical Education, Recreation, and Dance.

Patricia Holland is an Associate Professor in the department of educational leadership and cultural studies at the University of Houston. Her teaching and research interests focus on instructional supervision and teachers' professional development as essentially interpretive processes in which language is used to construct and examine the events of educational practice. Pat's publications include articles in the *American Educational Research Journal, Journal of Curriculum and Supervision, Peabody Journal of Education,* and *Journal of Curriculum Theorizing.* She

159

has also contributed chapters to several books, including *The Principal as Instructional Leader*, and *Commission, Reports & Reforms: Fashioning Educational Policy in the 1980's and Beyond.*

Marlene Johnson is a former Teacher of the Year for Katy Independent School District, Katy, Texas. She earned a bachelor's degree in Special Education from the University of Wisconsin-Oshkosh in the area of Mental Retardation and a master's degree from the University of Oregon-Eugene, with an emphasis in Learning Disabilities. After over twelve years as a regular and special educator, she completed a doctorate in curriculum and instruction at the University of Houston, focusing on leadership and teacher education. She has had experiences as research associate, student teacher supervisor, staff developer, and program supervisor. Marlene is presently functioning as an educational consultant in the Houston area.

Jane McCarthy is an Associate Professor in the department of instructional and curricular studies in the College of Education at the University of Nevada-Las Vegas. She also serves as the Director of the UNLV Accelerated Schools Satellite Center Project, affiliated with Stanford University. Jane previously served as the Director of the National Accelerated Schools Satellite Center Project at Stanford University. Prior to that she was on the faculty of the College of Education at the University of Houston where she served as the Chair of the instructional studies and teacher education program area. She was a member of the school board in Humble, Texas, where she held all offices, including that of President. Her research interests include effective teaching strategies for students in at-risk situations, school restructuring, and classroom management.